CONFESSIONS
of an
INDEPENDENT WOMAN

Truth, Lies, & Relationships

APRILLE FRANKS-HUNT

Unplugged with Dr. Tanya
Special Gift for a BEAUTIFUL person!
www.theconfessionsbook.com
@womenrecharged
@confessionsbook

Share your "Confessions" experience on Amazon with your review.

ISBN: 0615523412
ISBN-13: 9780615523415
Library of Congress Control Number:2011935987
Aprille Franks-Hunt, Norman, Oklahoma

DEDICATION

This book is dedicated to Women all over the world—
this is your time to use your authentic voice.

"In all my work what I try to say is that as human beings
we are more alike than we are unalike." Maya Angelou

ACKNOWLEDGMENTS

Thank God for bringing me this far and for all the blessings I have yet to receive.

With special thanks:

To my husband, Jessie for being supportive and the best friend a woman could have- late nights and crazy brainstorming sessions. I could not have done any of this without you. Lub'd ya's;)

To my kiddos, Maya & Ty, for being good kids and understanding the time I dedicated to complete this project.

To my parents for instilling me the strength to know that I can do all things and giving me inspiration to write this book. Through it all, I love you both.

To my friends for listening to my ranting over the last year about this book, Kita Hall, Sinita Wells, Terri Spinks, Lynn D. and Andrea Franklin and the rest of my Diva Escape Crew; Cheryl Wainwright, LaMara Stewart, and Brenda Garner.

To Monique Eddleton of Golden Parachutes Career Coaching in Atlanta, Georgia. Your guidance and insight led me in the right direction, solidifying everything that has happened this past year. My book is now a reality because of the "Spark" you put in me!

To Sharron Jackson, The BIS Coach, for supporting me through this process, cheering me along the way and becoming such a great friend.

To Alan Braadvedt, a great mentor and friend. I appreciate your input more than you may know.

To Tandra Brooks for being one of my biggest supporters and helping me the months before the release.

To all of the ladies and gents of Women Recharged who motivate me daily to do what I do and who continue to give my life a deeper purpose.

TABLE OF CONTENTS

ABOUT THE AUTHOR

Aprille Franks-Hunt is an author, speaker, life & business advisor, as well as a multi-faceted business professional, who walked away from a successful career to pursue her passion of inspiring women beyond motivation. Aprille is natural born leader and the Creator/CEO of Women Recharged, a powerful movement designed to spread the global message of transformation through Aprille's compelling LIVE, LEARN, and THRIVE mantra.

Aprille is also embedded in the business community consulting with small business owners, speaking at conferences, events and workshops. She also is an instructor at Metro Technology Center's business training department. Aprille's tenacity and determination also landed her first national speaking engagement on the stage of Women for Hire's CEO, Tory Johnson's Spark & Hustle Women's Business Conference in Atlanta, Ga. As a result she has been sought after by other organizations to deliver her candid messages to women on a vast array of topics. Aprille is also responsible for bringing the first edition of CRAVE, The Urban Girls Manifesto, a guide featuring women entrepreneurs, to Oklahoma.

She's the regular Monday night Co-Host on Oklahoma's own KSBI's, All About You, a live show dedicated to empowering and informing women. Additionally, she has been featured in several print publications and radio outlets for her business savvy.

Through all of these platforms, Aprille candidly shares her life experiences with honesty and transparency, revealing how it has helped her to become the woman she is today. She is passionately dedicated to the advancement of women personally and professionally. Her sassy, funny, down-to-earth style makes her the virtual best friend and advisor that every woman needs – when they are ready to embrace the truth. Aprille is an inspiration to many.

All of the events and people in this book are 100% factual.
The names of the people involved have been changed
to protect their identity, integrity and privacy.

WHY I WROTE THIS BOOK

Bossy, controlling, selfish, unreasonable, overbearing, belligerent, manly, demanding, and aggressive bitches. Wow. That's a little harsh—even for me to take. I have had enough of hearing those types of terms being used to describe women who have identified with the Independent Woman mantra. It's been the hot topic of main stream and social media forums, bloggers, beauty salons, barber shops, and your kitchen table heavily for the past three to five years. And not only is the term "independent woman" now super controversial, we've overcomplicated it. Putting the words strong, independent, successful, and woman together no longer works in the Love & Relationship department. Add Black to the equation and you just might have media frenzy on your hands – please unsubscribe to that notion as well.

But even with that being said I had to ask myself what was the root of this independence for me – and why I felt the need to identify with it so badly? Where was this coming from and why was this my proclamation? I had to dig deep and <u>own</u> some of the decisions I'd made in my past as it pertained to the relationships I had. I needed to be honest with myself in that, yes, sometimes I was in fact some of those words mentioned above. I was angry, defensive and had the ability to put up a wall that will intimidate most. But why – what's my backstory? Who am I and when did I lose myself? Lose myself – did I ever know myself? Was my proclamation a smokescreen for something else, a battle cry for something deeper?

Sure it was! But I was too busy being independent to hear my own voice. How could I expect to be whole within any relationship when I had my own demons to deal with? I couldn't – so I wrote this book to heal and to give other women a starting point to use their own voices. I want to start a real conversation about why we are the way we, own the decisions we've made and change course when we need too. I want each woman to own her own definition of who she is, when she is at her absolute best.

> If you have made mistakes, even serious ones, there is always another chance for you. What we call failure is not the falling down but the staying down. – Mary Pickford

This book isn't about the rhetoric we've been hearing in the media, finding a man or any of the mess we may have subscribed to. It's about truth. We have the power to change the way women are viewed in today's society but we first must be honest with ourselves. This is not a black, white or purple issue – this is a woman's issue, plain and simple.

I have opened my life up to the world in hopes to be a light through my imperfections. With that being said…

These are my real life confessions.

PART ONE

Off to a Rough Start

CHAPTER
1

THE CHOSEN ONE
CHOSEN FOR WHAT, THAT IS THE QUESTION

Childhood is not only the childhood we really had but also the impressions we formed of it in our adolescence and maturity. That is why childhood seems so long. Probably every period of life is multiplied by our reflections upon the next.

—CESARE PAVESE

Let me start out by saying I love my family. We are closer today than we have ever been but it wasn't always that way. It wasn't always roses and we didn't always like each other. With that being said, let's take a trip down history lane...

When I was ten years old, during a nice family game of monopoly while living in Harker Heights, Texas, my parents told me I was adopted. I didn't think too much about it at the time and it made sense as to why I didn't look like the rest of my immediate family. I remember saying to my mother, "you mean like Willis and Arnold?" And that was the end of that conversation for several years.

My biological mother, Lyn, had birthed three children by the time she was twenty. I was the third and only girl at the time—and for some reason, I was the one chosen to be placed for adoption. I was adopted through a private adoption; my godmother at the time and her husband adopted me and became my parents—Mary and Allen, the only parents I acknowledge and have known my entire life. Lyn went on to have eight more children, of which she kept them all. That was the one thing I could never really understand. Why me? That didn't start to mess with my mind until my early teen years. But I'll get to that soon enough.

Like most little girls, the men in my life growing up were my father, uncles, and grandfathers. They were there to serve as role models of what a man should be, demonstrating how men should conduct themselves and take care of their families. These men also impress upon us how men should treat the little girls that will one day become women. Women just like me, you, your mother, your sisters, and your girlfriends. So their involvement or lack thereof has more of a lasting impression on us than we might think. Our minds formulate what a man is, and these ideals are based on the actions or inactions of these men or other men in our lives growing up. It's our hope that those are good memories and the men were positive influences. But that's not always the case.

I must confess…

We were living at Fort Campbell, an army base near Clarksville, Tennessee, at the time. I was just three years old…and the funny thing is I remember *being* three years old. I recall that day like I'd remember so many others. It was bright and sunny outside, but inside it wasn't so bright.

There was an overturned ivory dining room table with chocolate brown swirls in it lying in the middle of my parents' dining room floor—they'd been fighting and my father flipped it over before he stormed out of the house, leaving my mother in distress. I recall seeing the wood-handled kitchen knife he stuffed in his back jeans pocket as he left out of the front door.

Even then, I was never afraid; fear wasn't something I felt when these situations between my parents turned toxic. It was something I suppressed early on. I was more curious and naturally upset at all the yelling. The older I got, as the abuse my father inflicted on my mother continued, I grew a huge disrespect for him and men in general, thinking to myself, "I don't need a man if this is what men do. Men hurt women. I'll pass." I never wanted to be afraid, I wanted to be strong. I didn't run and hide—I was usually right in the middle, yelling, "Leave my momma alone!"

We lived in Germany when I was just beginning kindergarten, my parents were young and active socially like most twenty something's. They were having a card game with some friends over this particular night, and, like many times before, my father had had too much to drink. Things got heated during the course of that game, and my father pushed my mother into a china cabinet. Glass shattered everywhere and us kids were sent to our rooms; the party was over.

I was afraid for my mother. No child wants to see their parent hurt, especially his or her mom. As I was in my bed trying hard to listen to what was going on in the next room, an angel appeared in the corner of my bedroom. It may sound strange to some, but God protects his children, and if he didn't, he sure protected me. I can recall vividly like it happened this morning. The angel told me not to be afraid and that I was safe. I knew then that there was something bigger than me and that I was safe no matter what was going on around me. I also realized at the young age of three that there was good and bad—and that I'd have to choose.

Fast forward several years of the same. One evening, while living in Killeen, Tx, my father started a fight with my mother over something trivial. Many times my mother was just protecting us. She rarely if ever provoked him, but he claimed she did. It was like walking on eggshells in your own home, not just for her, but for my little brother and me as well. Never knowing when he'd explode over the tiniest infraction. After hours of screaming and yelling, doors slamming, shattered glass, and drops of blood on the kitchen floor, my mother was hurt. She had a gash in her arm from the broken glass. She whisked us away to our neighbors, who lived just in the next duplex; you could literally throw a rock and hit their kitchen window. My mother ended up driving herself to the emergency room that night. I was furious at my father and a little afraid that he would come over to start some mess where we were. Not because he'd **do** something, but because it was embarrassing. Thankfully, he didn't. But little did I know that would be the least of my concerns that night.

The safe haven at the neighbors' house turned out to be anything but. To add fuel to the fire in an already volatile situation, our safe haven for the night turned into a hell for me. The son of our neighbor was home as well; we all went to school together. One of the brothers came into the room where I was sleeping and began to fondle me. I was molested by my neighbors' son that night. I woke from his touches but was too ashamed to stop him or yell for help. I tried moving in an attempt to "disturb" his movements, but nothing worked. He fingered me until he got his jollies off and left. I was a twelve-year-old virgin at the time and wasn't even thinking about boys in this manner. I wanted to die in my sleep after he left the room, but I didn't. I lay there trying to make sense of what had just happened. When I woke the next morning, I cornered him and told him I was going to tell his mother what he'd done. I'll never forget what he said to me with a deviant look on his face...

"I don't know **what** you're talking about."

"You don't know what I'm talking about!?" I aggressively whispered. "You came in my room last night, you know what you did!"

I was too embarrassed to even repeat it to him. I was thinking I hated him and we don't need boys or men for anything. I didn't tell his mother because I didn't want her to think it was my fault, and I was ashamed. I didn't tell **my** mother because she was already dealing with her own issues from the previous night with my father. I didn't want to add stress to her. In the big scheme of things, it just didn't seem that important. So I dealt with it, well, kind of. Moving on…

My mother wasn't alone in her abuse. Before my grandfather, on my father's side, passed away, he was also abusive to my grandmother for what seemed like no reason at all. Not that there is ever a good reason. He was also an alcoholic. I have found that alcoholics have a warped sense of reality. *And now it's a disease…I guess smoking is a disease too—I never understood how voluntary damage to your body becomes the disease rather than causing diseases.* I specifically recall one incident in particular when my grandfather kicked us kids out of the house to play Russian roulette with my grandmother. My aunts, uncle, little brother and I were all afraid for her.

I loved my grandfather, and he was never abusive to me, but he caused my grandmother so much pain. I never understood why this was happening, but it appeared to be normal to them. My father was doing it and my mother was putting up with it. My grandfather was doing it to my grandmother, and she put up with it, too. Still, I knew it wasn't right because of the pain and humiliation I saw in their faces. As I got older, I never understood why they didn't fight back or just leave. And it wasn't until just recently when I spoke to my mother about this that I understood: it was for the protection of my brother and me that she stayed. Women in that generation weren't from the world we are today. Many women didn't leave and lived in silence. They didn't know to fight back, so they just didn't.

As my brother and I grew older, the physical fighting between my parents began to diminish as my mother began standing up for herself. Not only my mother, but we also were more vocal with what we'd do to our father if he were to "put his hands" on our mother again. We were not little kids anymore—we could stick up for her in a major way. We'd get in his face anytime he thought he wanted to be a little too aggressive with her. Something about alcoholics is that they never remember the pain they cause—probably one of the worst characteristics about them. They'll wreak havoc on you and terrorize you in one instance, then not remember a damn thing the next day, expecting you to act as if everything is normal. Meanwhile, you have emotional and physical battle scars from the night, days or years before. I couldn't stand for it any longer and was never afraid to confront him. As a young teenager, *that* created a lot of problems in our household. He couldn't tell me anything—I couldn't trust him. Even when I was wrong, I didn't respect his discipline because he didn't respect my mother. This made most of what my father said to me null and void. Not a good thing.

By the time I reached my high school years, I had a nasty attitude in general, a rocky relationship with my mother, and basically no relationship with my father. My brother and I were not close either; I just existed in the household. I was angry—in fact, my parents thought I was crazy, but I was far from it. And because I was acting out, they sent me to counseling. I wonder, did it ever occur to them that **they** were the problem? I think they forgot I was a person, and my mother forgot or didn't realize the impact our environment was having on my attitude. What did I really have to be happy about? I think parents forget that their messed-up situations affect us (as children) no matter what they tell us we should be doing. We pay more attention to actions and reactions, not words alone. Thinking back, I think I wanted my mother to leave my father so we'd be happier. At least the fighting would stop—after all, you can't fight a battle without any participants. It wasn't that we didn't love our father, but he sure as hell didn't make it easy.

As the years progressed those memories didn't just dissipate. As I grew into my young adulthood, they remained with me, bottled up. I was dead set on one fact: men cannot be trusted, period. I didn't need one if in one moment you can be the best thing in the world to them and in the next they can violate you in some way that would hurt you or break your spirit. Is this what love and marriage are about? Hurt and pain, anguish, with a few good times sprinkled in here and there? Maybe a little temporary happiness to soothe the pain. There has to be something better than that, something more. Because if that's the case, I'll learn to do all the things a man should do on my own – it can't be that hard.

Early on I had the mind-set that independence would be my only companion even before I knew what the word stood for. I wanted out of the house, to have my own place, my own family, and to earn my own money. There really were no other options. I wanted my own voice. I knew that if something went wrong in my life, I didn't want a man to be responsible for it. I saw what they were capable of doing to women they claimed they loved. And I refused to be one of "those" women. I wouldn't allow *that* to happen to me. I'd be in control and take care of myself. Sigh. Even with those thoughts and feelings I still wanted attention that only a man could give me, to be love in only a way that I wasn't sure existed.

CHAPTER
2

DIRTY OLD MAN

TRICKS AREN'T FOR KIDS

If I am not good to myself,
how can I expect anyone else to be good to me?

— MAYA ANGELOU

At sixteen, I was searching for something. I didn't have any real focus on the present; I just wanted to make it to the future. I knew whatever the future held, it had to be better than the damage I was doing to myself and that **had** been done to me. It's hard to admit, but I didn't think about why I did some of the things I did; I just did them knowing I'd have to suffer the consequences later. From skipping school to sleeping around, I was trying to figure me out. Who am I and what is my purpose? Not as deep as my purpose now, back then I just wondered why I was alive when life didn't seem so great. Back then, I didn't realize I was looking to fill a void, but subconsciously I was. Any attention was good, even when it wasn't.

My promiscuity landed me in a lot of trouble. Meaningful sex at that age didn't exist. I can recall many occasions when I'd have sex just to have sex—no meaning or connection was needed; I wanted the affection, the touch. It was odd; I never really trusted or believed anything the boys my age told me, but I wanted to. I wanted to be pretty, popular, and liked. And loved and touched in a way that I thought represented love, hoping it would make me feel better about myself. But it didn't and never has. It would be ten years before I realize this.

I needed to be validated and wanted acceptance by my parents and peers. I knew somewhere deep down I was a good person. But I didn't value myself in the way I expected others to value me. I felt unattractive and a little awkward. I held their thoughts and perceptions of me to a higher standard than I actually held for myself. I knew I had something special but was too naïve to tap into it.

I must confess…

School was boring me; I wasn't the best student though I was very smart. I wanted to be out on my own—to get on with my life. This particular day I was being punished for skipping school. I felt as though I was wasting my time and figured I knew everything I would learn in high school anyway. At the time my mother was working as a nurse's aide at a nursing home near our house. So, you guessed it, my punishment was a month volunteering at the nursing home on the weekends. At first I dreaded it; I was afraid of old people like men are afraid to pick up newborn babies. But as soon as I started volunteering there, I made some of the best friends a teenage girl will ever have. If you want advice, ask any woman in her right mind over the age of sixty-five if she can tell you a thing or two about life that your mother didn't have the courage to say.

It's Mardi Gras in Mobile, 1991. The streets were filled with people from near and far, old and young, black and white, all screaming at the passing floats. All the food, drinks, alcohol, MoonPies, and, yes, colored beads any one person could handle! Only we yell for beads in Mobile and have a no-flashing rule! It's Saturday, a typical day at the nursing home, helping patients, combing their hair, reading them the paper, and laughing with them at the stories from their younger years. It's also the weekend before Fat Tuesday, Mardi Gras day. A group of well-known, established fraternity brothers walked in totally decked out in their Mardi Gras costumes, masks, and colored beads. Their group was being led in by an older, distinguished gentleman. They were giving back to the community and performing an in-house parade for the patients. Getting those beads, hearing the music, dancing, and the extra attention just put a smile on their faces. The patients of the home thoroughly enjoyed themselves and so did I.

There was one guy in particular that I noticed, and mercy, was he the cutest guy I had ever seen. He was extremely attractive and out of my league, for sure. I mean, he's attending college and a member of a very popular fraternity. I don't have a chance, I thought to myself. I was just a sophomore, barely in high school. I saw the other guys with him, but he was by far the most intriguing. A girl can dream!

When the parade was nearly over, to my surprise the guy I had my eye on stopped to talk to me as I was sitting near the entrance.

"Hey, how are you? What are you doing here?" he asked.

"I'm fine, just volunteering," I replied nervously.

"That's cool. Our fraternity does this every year, and we do other things within the community as well," he said.

"That's pretty cool; looks like the patients really enjoyed it! What's your name?" I said to him.

"Troy."

"Hi, I'm April," I said.

All I could think is, "oh my goodness, he's actually talking to me! Me, a high school sophomore talking to a college boy." After a little small talk, he asked for my number. Troy was still too old for my parents' comfort level for dating, so I wasn't sure how we were going to see each other in reality, but the idea of it was nice. I wasn't allowed to date because my parents didn't trust me. Though I was excited about our encounter, I knew my mother wouldn't be, so I took his number. I didn't want him calling the house for fear of my parents grilling me. This was the pager era and ten pound cell phones had just come out—and I had neither.

I waited a couple of weeks before I called him. The ball was in my court—I didn't want to wait too long and risk the chance of him forgetting who I was, so I called him one day from school during lunch.

"Hello, may I speak to Troy?" I asked nervously.

"This is him," said a voice.

"You don't sound like yourself," I said to him.

I'm thinking he sounded a little different from when we met, but I had the right name and number, so it was all good.

"This is Troy. I saw you at the nursing home," he reassured me.

"Oh, OK, cool. My cousin, Lele, and I were thinking about ditching the rest of the day. What are you up to?" I asked.

I didn't have any expectations at all. I just wanted to see him again, get to know him, and hang out. It was common practice for many of the students to skip classes and hang out with older friends or siblings that were in college. I was no different.

"Nothing much, come on over," he said.

"Can you pick us up from school?"

"Take a cab. I'll leave the fare on the table in the foyer, just run in and get it. My address is 213 Axe Avenue."

"OK, see you in a bit," I said as I hung up the pay phone.

Well, that was easy. He still remembered me and wanted to see me again. It was a quick ten-minute cab ride over, and we pulled up in front of a nice two-story brick house. I ran inside and, just as Troy said, the door was unlocked and the cab fare was sitting on the table in the foyer, waiting for me. My cousin and I paid, tipped the cabbie and off inside we went.

"Heeeeelloooo," I sang as we were walking inside.

"I'm upstairs, just come up," the voice said.

I got to the top of the landing and heard a TV playing, so I peeked into the room it was coming from but only saw a familiar-looking older man. "Whoops," I thought, and looked into another opened door. No one was there, so I said to the man:

"Where's Troy?"

"I'm Troy," he said.

"Umm, you're not the guy I met at the nursin…" I began to say.

"Come sit next to me," he interrupted, signaling me to sit next to him on the bed as he's patting his hand on bed.

With a puzzled look on my face, I hesitantly went into the bedroom and slowly slid down onto the opposite corner of the bed from where he was sitting. What kind of craziness is this I thought to myself? Did I just get tricked into coming over here by some old man? I do remember seeing him at the nursing home. He was the distinguished gentleman leading the younger frat guys during the Mardi Gras parade. And he was handsome in an *old man knocking on forty kind of way*. My heart was beating fast and for a moment I felt trapped.

"Troy is my son; I'm his father."

To keep this simple, let's call the father, Doc, and the son is Troy.

"Who did I speak to on the phone?" I asked.

"That was me; Troy is away at college—four hours away. He attends Alabama A&M in Huntsville," he explained. "But you don't want him, he doesn't have any money. What he gets, he gets from me, and I'm right here."

I am sure I had a dumb, naïve look on my face. Money? Who said anything about that and why would he just give me any money? Oh my goodness, at sixteen years old I wasn't thinking about a man with money at all. Hell, I wasn't thinking about a *grown* man in the first place. Ew, he was old enough to be my dad. I just wanted what most girls my age wanted: to be popular in high school, and for my mom and me to get along, and maybe a cute boyfriend on the football team. You know, typical sixteen-year-old girl stuff.

Lele was in the media room just hanging out watching TV as she waited for me to tell her what in the heck was going on. I went in and told her in a wide-eyed whisper, "That's not him, that's his dad!" I was feeling kind of scared, but not scared enough to run out of there, so I went back into the room and kept talking to him. I felt obligated because he was old enough to be my father; besides, we were stuck.

He showed us around the house, and it *was* beautiful. My cousin Lele and I were looking at each other like, "wow." He showed us his fully stocked bar with liquors we'd never heard of and most we didn't even know how to mix properly. He fixed us both a drink and we just talked for a while downstairs in the dining area. We knew there would be no rules and no parents to take orders from if we did come back. After a couple of hours, Lele and I had to get going. He gave me something like $40 then took us back to school so we could catch the bus home. I was in amazement and nervous at the same time.

After that first visit I don't think I thought of going back. But there were times when I felt I needed to hide, and so I did. Curiosity must have a huge cat cemetery somewhere, because it sure got the best of me. I just wanted to be free. I wanted to know what this older man was about—why he wanted me and what were these things, in his words, he "could do" for me that he kept speaking of. The control was intoxicating; the power was misleading, and the unknown was kind of exciting. I was like a kid in a candy store, but much bigger, and the stakes were higher.

Doc was a tall, handsome, caramel coated, and a very charismatic man. He was (and still is) a well-known, respected businessman and a community leader living in the South. At that time, with a passion for screwing young high school girls; I pray times have changed for him. I'm not sure if or in what way I was attracted to him. Maybe it was his perceived power. He wanted to show me things that a boy my age couldn't show me or didn't even know existed. Though I was naïve, I can't pretend that I didn't know what I was about to do. I'm not sure if I signed up for it, or if I was drafted. I was confused.

So, exactly what was the attraction between a thirty-nine-year-old man and the sixteen-year-old girl who was supposed to be *interested* in his son? My sixteen-year-old answer was, "I'm mature for my age, and he just likes younger women." My now thirty-five-plus-something-year-old answer is, "He was a pedophile," point blank. He wanted to control and dominate me. He tricked me and then enticed me with things, and to a degree I allowed him to. He was a very sweet man. Doc liked the control in every aspect, but he was never possessive-controlling crazy with me. He never interfered or even showed he cared about attention I got from other boys from school. It never even came up. He just wanted me to do what he wanted me to do when I was with him. Thinking back, I don't think he cared about me at all; it was just give and take. I was a commodity to be used when he needed me. He taught me that my body was a bargaining tool and, if used properly, I could have anything I wanted from a man.

And just like that, the next couple of years of my life went quickly. I learned a lot; maybe too much, too soon. Though I am no longer that young girl, I am her, and she was me. He molded me emotionally and sexually into what he wanted me to be. I didn't feel like he was a father figure, but I respected him as if he were. I knew what we were doing was wrong because I was smart enough not to tell a soul. The only person that knew initially was my cousin Lele.

Now, I wasn't a virgin at this point, but I wasn't *that* experienced either. Sure I had had sex with the boys my age in the past, but that was very different than the type of sex Doc and I had. He wasn't just on top of me pumping his hips. We weren't in love, but there was a lot of lovemaking going on. That's what he called it. It was never just sex. He'd say, "Give me some lovin', girl." Makes me sick to my stomach just thinking about it now, especially since I have a sixteen-year-old daughter myself (Shania).

I can remember calling him to ask for clothes, make up, pocket money or whatever and he'd always ask me, "When do you have time to come over?"

I knew ex—actly what that meant. I'd have to give him some "lovin' " in order to get whatever I was asking him for. I hated it but I still fell for it many times. I'd walk in, head right to the bar, and fix myself a cocktail. He was almost always home during the day. I should have been in school, but I wasn't on many occasions. So up the stairs I'd go, and off with my clothes by the time I got to the bedroom. It didn't start out that aggressive and straight to the point, but I learned quickly; it was a progression over time. Most kids will do what you tell them; if you keep telling them to do the same thing, they'll keep doing it. On occasions he'd be playing porn when I arrived; I didn't understand the obsession with it at the time. But he wanted me to be into it, he wanted me to watch it, he wanted me to like it, and so I pretended I did. I never argued with him. There were countless sexual encounters with Doc. Each time brought the introduction of something new to try, to do, to touch, to feel. Intoxicating to my young soul.

After a couple of months had gone by, I phoned Doc for a visit. Oddly, Troy, the son, answered the phone. In retrospect it wasn't so odd; he was a college kid visiting his father for spring break. I was stunned but kept my cool and just asked how he was doing, followed by some small talk about school. He implied he wanted to see me, and my stomach turned in that moment. "Sure, we can see each other," I said with hesitation.

I didn't know what else to say. I mean, why else would I be calling his father's house after I hadn't heard from Troy since we had met months ago during Mardi Gras? I didn't want to see him but I was so weak. I knew I was about to go someplace I didn't want to go, but I felt as thought I didn't have a choice. My bags were already packed. I had already made my bed.

Then, out of the blue, he asked me, "Has my dad ever hit on you?"

"No! Why would you say something like that?" I responded with a raised brow.

"He's done that in the past, taken my girlfriends, so I was just wondering," he said nonchalantly.

"Your dad, umm, no!" I exclaimed. "What time will you be here to pick me up?"

I couldn't believe he'd asked me that. I lied to him and acted like that was the most absurd thing he could ask me.

Troy picked me up from school, and off we went to hang out with his other college friends for a bit. I wanted to know where Doc was, just in case he wanted to go home. Sure enough, after hanging out, he wanted to go home before heading back on the road to Huntsville. I knew he was going to try to get me to have sex with him and honestly I just wanted to go home—imagine that.

"Will we be alone?" I asked him.

"I dunno, my dad might be home," he said cheerfully.

Dammit, I thought. And why on earth is he so excited? This isn't good. I've gotten myself into a mess—again. At first, getting to know Troy was the goal, which would have just been marvelous! Just to hang out with a fine college guy, maybe even date him exclusively. But that would never happen now. I am screwing his father. Talk about feeling low.

How would this work out? It wouldn't, that's how. Either way, I didn't want the drama or confrontation. I didn't want to be with Troy, either, since I had already met Doc. I mean, what would be the point of that? But this day I was going to come in contact with them both at the same time, and I knew it.

We soon arrived at the house and inside we went. He introduced me to his dad and we (Doc and I) both acted like it was the first time we'd ever laid eyes on each other. We shook hands like strangers and played the whole "nice to meet you" bit. Talk about playing a game—checkmate. Again, he was teaching me something still every step of the way.

As we walked away, I could feel Doc's eyes on the back of my neck. Troy and I headed upstairs to his bedroom. Troy wanted to have sex but I *really* didn't. For some reason I felt obligated to sleep with him. Why? I ask myself. I don't even know why I was afraid to say no to him. All I could think of was that his dad, Doc, was in the house, and what if he could see or hear us! I'm disgusted with myself right now. I gave in and had sex with Troy because I was afraid to say no; allowing myself to be used. It wasn't that I wanted it, because I didn't. I found myself doing stupid things just to be doing stupid things—just to regret them later. I said a prayer to myself:

"God, if you get me outta this mess, I promise I won't have sex until I'm married."

I don't even think God hears those "if you do this, I'll promise not to do that" calls made out of desperation. But that was all I had at the time.

As I was hanging off the bed, Troy was on top of me, just pumping to getting his jollies off, and all I could think was "please hurry up" as I was staring at the ceiling. I felt like a puppy in a puppy mill; just there to get screwed and passed on. I had learned to disconnect during sex. What happened next? I noticed the bedroom door was NOT closed all the way. And the draft from the air conditioning had pushed it open enough to peek in or out. I was totally out of sorts and wanted this sexual waste of time to be over. And soon enough it was—but not before Doc came upstairs and peeked in the door as his son was screwing me. Ashamed, ashamed, ashamed I was. I wanted out of there so badly. God, just strike me down right now.

Of course, Troy had just gotten what he wanted from me and was packing up to head back on the road. He didn't have time to take me home and suggested his dad, Doc, take me home as a favor to him. I felt sick, again.

"Dad, can you take April home for me? I gotta head out!" Troy asked.

"Sure, no problem," Doc said with a sly grin.

My stomach was turning at the thought. Maybe an hour later Troy was gone, and this would be the last time I ever spoke to him. I was now alone in the house with Doc and I felt as low as I should have.

Doc then had the audacity to ask me:

"Has my son ever asked you about me?"

"Yes," I said.

"And what did you tell him?" he asked.

"Nothing, nothing at all," I said in disbelief with a peculiar look on my face.

Now, why would he ask me that? I wondered. I mean, he was wrong from the start. He knew when I met his son and where. He knew he tricked me into coming over the first time. He knew he'd been manipulating our "relationship," and I use the term oh so loosely, from the start. Troy was the one in the dark. Then, to make matters worse, he had the nerve to utter:

"Who's better in bed?"

"What!" I yelled.

"Whose sex is better, me or my son?" he repeated.

Now I wanted to break down and cry, but I got myself in this mess, so I answered because now he was waiting for me to say HIM. At that time I didn't think for a moment that they had planned this all out. That would be cruel and wrong on so many levels. So I said, "Yours." Now I was playing the game back.

This was just the beginning—only a few months in. Of course, I asked myself several times why I kept going back. The truth was, he had my mind from the beginning, and once I got to know him better, he was a nice person, and as time went on a part of me didn't want it to stop. I was beginning to get used to it. The money, the freedom, the alcohol, and the unknown were all appetizing. This had to be all a part of his molding me into what he wanted. It was the introduction of all the things I should have learned in my twenties and some of it maybe not at all. I was barely sixteen, but mentally I was much older.

Occasionally my friends and I would go there to hang out, and he'd have his way with them if he wanted them too. I felt so guilty about that; even though he never forced himself of any of us, I took them over there. There were no threesome encounters between us girls, but he certainly controlled the situation. Mutually, between them the attraction was always what he had or whatever he thought would lure them in. It didn't matter to them or him, and I found myself being pissed that he would have sex with my friends. They never said no because he was like a "free pass" to adulthood or something. Like I said, no rules. I was a child in his eyes, and so were they; he didn't need my permission to do anything. This was his motive and he knew how to play it. Very manipulative. I'm thinking he dealt with young girls because I doubt that grown women would have gone for his game. But knowing what I know now about grown women, perhaps they would have. He had a long term girlfriend of 14 years and I doubt she had a clue—but again, who knows.

The "thing" between Doc and me went on for about three years off and on. I want to say that I knew better all along, but I'm not sure if I truly did. I can admit I went back to him over and over again of my own free will.

Eventually, Doc told me that his son knew I had been sleeping with him the entire time. I felt so low, sucker punched. He used me up and I kinda let him. In retrospect, I think this was their game. It's my guess that Doc would use his son to prey on young women—and they'd have their way, I can only speculate—knowing his father would step in...and take over to fulfill his fantasies. This is what he was being taught—I used to wonder what kind of man Troy turned out to be.

From that point I vowed that never again would I allow a man to use, abuse, or manipulate me. I won't do things I don't want to, I'll say **no** when I mean *no*. I'll be smarter, stronger, and be in charge of my own life. I don't need a man if this is what they do. I can't stand being tricked, manipulated, or controlled in any way. I'll stick up for myself—and have the freedom to not depend on anyone for anything. I knew I was better than the type of decisions I kept making. I have to do better, I'd say to myself. I was too smart to keep going down the wrong roads. I needed guidance and I wasn't getting it but I knew where to start—church.

I began making church a routine part of my life. At eighteen years old, I first heard my pastor say to write down the things I wanted in life—including the type of man I wanted. He reminded me that "I" deserved the very best. Those were words I **wanted** to believe: that by making this list, God would send me the perfect man in the perfect situation. But even with my new attitude, I questioned, why did I suddenly deserve the best? I hadn't earned it, I wasn't worthy of it, nor did I know what the "best" was. Either way, I did what I was told and made my list. These would be my new standards to live by—or would they.

CHAPTER
3

BITTERNESS IS REAL
BUT IT AIN'T SEXY

You will not be punished for your anger,
you will be punished by your anger.

—BUDDHA

Life has its way of happening to all of us. Sometimes we get into a mess on our own, and other times it just seems to find us. Oftentimes, we're not ready or even expecting its little hiccups. We could be coasting along quite nicely and then we suddenly derail.

When was the last time you woke up and said, "I think I want my heart broken today" or "I wish something would go just the opposite of what I'm expecting"? Just so you can spend months pissed off, and years being bitter and asking God why this mess happened to you. Unless you enjoy inflicting anguish and pain on yourself, chances are, that's not a fantasy you envisioned. But life happens, and while it may not be anything you would have imagined, you're left standing to deal with it. The feelings of denial, rejection, shame, guilt, and numbness are all things associated with being bitter and angry. Whether the root was born from your childhood, your environment, abuse, or by circumstances, it is fed by your despair; you allowed bitterness to take residence in your heart and mind. When you're so angry about "that situation," all you see is red. Sometimes you just can't help but to go there kicking and screaming the entire time.

At some point we've all been bitter towards someone who has wronged us or we felt has wronged us in some way. You may have every right in the world to be hurt and feel the way you do about someone or some situation but you don't want it taking root in your life. It's self- defeating, eating you from the inside out, fueled by your inability or unwillingness to let go and forgive. It's not where you want to be, but a reality none the less.

No one understands you or how you're feeling. Nothing is good enough, not a man or a new situation. Not even your closest of girlfriends can carry on a decent conversation with you, because every other word out of your mouth is a negative one. The amount of energy that being bitter requires can drain the light from the sun, or put people in a position not to want to deal with or be around you. As the old saying goes, 'misery loves company'. And even through your dating attempts, men can sense bitterness. They can smell it a mile away and read it through your online dating profiles, messages, and telephone conversations. Bitterness is an emotion that will send you in a downward spiral of self-pity. It will leave you there to wallow in it. But sometimes it's out of your control.

I must confess...

I was on a celibacy journey and wanted to figure out who I was without the influence of a man in my life sexually. I had gone about eight weeks without, which was a long time for me. I knew there was something in me that was great—I just needed to be *still* long enough to recognize it. I was in the mode of not wanting to be remotely entertained by any man. But this week was going to be a long one.

It's Monday

I'm nineteen years old and have been set up on a blind date I don't want to go on, but my neighbor insists. The guy she knows is too great for me to pass up, she says. So I agree after a week of her getting on my nerves to meet this man.

Living on the second floor; I see him pull up in his dark blue four-door Oldsmobile. Knock, knock at the door. I am a little nervous as I head to the door. Good nervous, antsy even. I open the door and there stands a six-foot-three, 245-pound, handsome, chocolate, well-built man with a nice smile. He even looks like he can pick me up—always a side thought I have. Something about a man that can pick you up, with or without your clothes on, is just, well, sexy as hell. Both of us are smiling from ear to ear as we give each other a welcome hug.

I invite him in, fix us a cocktail, then we talk for four or five hours right in my living room (on my floral loveseat, to be exact). It is one of those perfect moments you have with a guy you've just met. The moment where you can totally contradict yourself into thinking how great he must be but then think how screwed up he could be in the same thought. Always looking for flaws and reasons not to see him again because he can't be this nice, this sweet, and this perfect.

But even I have to admit, it is refreshing to have some nice convo; kids, past relationships, careers, and my eight-week celibacy stint—he seems to be interested and tells me he is in the same place in his life and he just wants to take things slow. After the last few years I've had, taking it slow sounds real good to me.

It's Tuesday

I have a flutter in my stomach, waiting for the phone to ring. The anticipation is what keeps it exciting. I love it when a man calls or shows me that I'm on his mind without me having to initiate it. We talk a couple of times throughout the day about absolutely nothing. How sweet it is.

It's Wednesday

He calls and wants to see me—I tell him I am at the Laundromat and could we meet up a little later if he wants. Daniel lets me know he has to work later but just wants to see me for a little bit and offers to come where I am. I think, OK, he must really like me.

> Over analyzing every little detail = guilty. Why do we do that? Really, he must like me because he stopped at the Laundromat on the way to work? Lord help the day.

Half an hour later there he is, helping me with my laundry. Now what woman wouldn't want that and a single parent too? Think back to nineteen—men that age aren't helping with your dirty laundry—they just want to *dirty your laundry*. We chat a bit, he gives me $15 and a nice hug, and off he goes. Now I am thinking, this is good; I could really like this guy. Sure, $15 may seem like chump change, but that's a full tank of gas for my '87 Nissan Sentra and a meal deal at somebody's fast food restaurant.

It's Thursday

We talk a couple of times and make a date for the next day, Friday. We'll do dinner at Red Lobster, and then head over to my cousin Roxy's apartment—she lives just five minutes away—for a card party afterwards.

It's Friday

After working my day shift at McDonald's, it's time to get ready for my date. It's the perfect beginning of the weekend, a date with my Daniel! Besides, it's been a great week getting to know him so far. Hair, nails, and new outfit—check, check, and check!

Seven o'clock can't come fast enough. Daniel comes to the door, and off we go. He looks great and smells even better. Red Lobster, yummy, those garlic biscuits are my favorite. I can eat like five of them. I have the Cajun shrimp pasta and he has the special of the day. We are really enjoying each other's company, laughing, talking, and giving each other the "I think I like you" eyes. I remember thinking how nice this is and that I want to keep it going. After a couple of hours, we leave the restaurant and head to the liquor store to get something to take to Roxy's party. I never show up at someone's house without a bottle of wine, dessert, or something; it's just proper.

As we approach the door of the apartment, we can hear Tupac playing from the stairs. Roxy loves Tupac, we all do. I introduce Daniel to her and to her fling at the time. Drinks are being consumed and the card party is in full swing. I am so glad Roxy lives right next door in a neighboring complex so when the party is over we will be back at my place in less than five minutes. Several hours later we head back to my apartment with baby Shania in tow around 1 a.m. or so.

Daniel and I both have had several drinks at Roxy's, so I know he is in no position to drive. After putting the baby in her room, again we talk until about 3:40 a.m., long enough to sober up and get some sleep, or so I think. I wear a blue/white flannel gown and white granny panties to bed. Though it has only been a few days, I feel comfortable with him in my home. He is like a protector, ya know, the kind of man that when he hugs you, you really feel safe in his arms. He seems sincere.

"You can stay, just turn off the lights and TV before going to sleep," I say to him as I walk down the hall to my bedroom.

I don't think anything of it because…well, I don't know why. I just can't wait to go to bed; it's been a long day at work, running around afterwards, and then getting ready for our date. Going to Roxy's was the icing on the cake. I hit the bed so hard I can't even remember drifting off to sleep.

Totally Blind-sighted

I feel something wet and cool on the bottom of my back. I awaken in a daze to find Daniel licking my lower back near my butt! I quickly turn over, sit up, and yell, "What the hell are you doing?!"

I will never, never forget what he said to me after that.

"You're gonna give me this pussy!" he demands.

I can't believe this is happening to me. All I can think is, *I am not going to be raped right now with my daughter in the next room. And I did everything right—why would he want to do this?* The power struggle begins. All I can say is, "NO, NO, NO, PLEASE, pleeeeease DON'T do this!" as I yell, squirming to keep my panties on.

My five-foot-eight, 145-pound frame is no match for his six-foot-three, 245-pound athletically built body. It's only been a few minutes, but I am losing the power struggle. He puts his hand over my mouth and says, "All the shit I've done for you, you're gonna give me this pussy!" in a demonic voice.

It is like this isn't him. His voice is *totally* different, as if <u>he is</u> possessed. I will never forget it for as long as I live. I know in this moment that he has lost his damn mind, there *is* a stranger in my house, and I am going to be raped.

He looks me in my eyes as he shoves his penis inside me and begins to thrust—raping me. In that moment I just close my eyes and cry, praying for it to be over soon; I am screaming to the top of my lungs on the inside for help. But no one can hear me. Tears run from my eyes and into my ears as if I am under water. This is not happening, this is not happening, this is not happening, I think. But the truth is, it **is** happening. He is inside me for the longest few minutes, which seem like an hour, of my life. It's just like in the movies when everything moves in slow motion. Everything around me is muffled, nothing is clear. He ejaculates inside me, looks me in my eyes, and then says, "Oh, my God, what have I done?"

I scream, "You raped me, get the fuck off me!"

He jumps off me and literally runs down the hall and out of my apartment, leaving the door to my apartment wide open. I climb out of bed and run to the bathroom to wipe as much of him *out* of me as possible. I run to the kitchen, grab a knife, and run after him; down the stairs, and into the parking lot. My split-second plan is to stab his tires so he can't run from the police. He'll be forced to face the police—but the rapist, coward; piece of shit is already gone.

As I stand there like a madwoman, standing half naked in the parking lot with a knife in my hand, I am in disbelief that **this** has even happened to me. I was making changes for the better. I mean, I had standards. I was honest with him and wasn't having sex with anyone. He fit the paper-perfect version of what a man should be up until that point. He was supposed to be a nice guy.

I go back to my apartment to call 911. My older brother lives in the same complex so I call him and tell him what happened. He comes over and takes my baby home with him; she had no idea what was going on. I thank God she slept through the entire ordeal.

Once the police arrive, the investigator takes pictures of my bedroom and I give my statement. Off to the hospital I go with the sergeant. Understand the anger I feel at myself for being so stupid as to trust this man and to have him in my home. Why would I let him sleep over? I mean, I barely know him, really. I don't know anything about him aside from what he told me. I am so pissed for allowing him to prey upon me and break my own vow of "me time." God, how could I be so gullible? And what would possess him to force himself on me? He wasn't drunk or high—he was in his right mind.

The sergeant and I finally arrive at the hospital after about forty minutes. They proceed to do a rape kit, which by the way will make you feel like a victim even when you are trying hard not to. The two most unforgettable parts of that process are how they scalp both sides of my hair near my hairline, then give me a shot and the morning-after pill just in case I have become pregnant or gotten some sexually transmitted disease. The thought of either really pisses me off. I thank God for modern medicine; so I never have to find out.

"Would you like to press charges?" asks the sergeant.

"YES!" I cry.

I don't even have to think about it. How could I not press charges! I can't believe I am a victim of rape. How demoralizing. How shameful to even say the words, "I've been raped." What a violation of everything in me. I can't believe, as smart, strong, and independent as I am, that this is happening...to me. I've been doing pretty good, working full time, and taking care of myself and Shania on my own. To make matters more shameful—my mother and god mother came to the emergency room to see me. Who wants to say the words...*I've been raped*? Friday—is a real bad day.

The Morning(s) After

I'd been in a boxing match with a rapist and my body felt like it. I was sore from my inner thighs to other muscles I didn't even know I had. How could I walk outside my apartment and face people? Not that everyone knew, but it seemed like they did, and my brother had a big mouth. Had I known I was in the company of a rapist, he'd never made it past the threshold of my apartment. I would have never entertained him. For all I knew he could have been a murderer.

At that time the only two women, who were close to me, were Anne and my cousin Roxy. I called to tell them what had happened so I could cry it out, scream about it, and exert any other emotions I had. And what happened next, I couldn't believe. They doubted me, as if I had made it up. I was thinking, "What in the hell is going on?" I'd always been honest with them, always. Anne was the pathological liar, but that's another story. We were a trio; see one of us and you'd see the other two coming. Now, I'll be the first to admit, I had been promiscuous and enjoyed sex but on my terms and when I wanted it. There had been plenty of occasions when a man wanted some, I said NO, and he just went on his way. Never had anyone tried, much less attempted, to actually "take" some from me. I mean to go as far as to rape me…

Initially, I think it was too much for my friends to deal with; no words, no thoughts, and no actions. Just disbelief—this doesn't happen in *our* community. We don't scream "rape." You must have done something, said something, or worn something provocative. Surely, I must have teased him or led him on.

Our friendship was never the same after that.

I was broken, angry, and I wanted him to die slowly from the inside out. I wanted him to hurt and feel humiliated the way I did. I wanted him to be known as the rapist he was. Court was coming up in a couple of weeks, so I just focused on justice being served. I would prevail; after all, I was the one who had gotten raped.

Anne went to court with me; it was early in the morning. I stood there and let my court-appointed, waste-of-taxpayer-money attorney do the talking. Daniel stood there with eyeglasses on, trying to appear intelligent. He had hired an attorney—a good one. It was a woman long blonde hair—she tore me alive. They claimed that we had sex the first time we met and that I was a whore trying to ruin his good name! I didn't even know where that misguided notion had come from. I didn't want a thing from him; I was in a totally different space in my life.

> The abuse from the justice system was almost as bad as being raped. The case wasn't about what's right or the truth. It's about proof and if you can prove a lie…that's justice.

"We didn't have sex, we never had sex, and he raped me! How can you defend him, he's guilty! What is wrong with you?" I pled to his attorney.

But, on the contrary, he wasn't guilty in a court of law. Isn't that something? He raped me and he *wasn't* guilty. Instead, I was attacked, accused of being the predator by his attorney. He and I both knew he was lying. But none of the truth mattered. I had to prove it! I was so enraged. Let me say that again: he raped me and I had to fight him off of me, in my apartment, with my baby in the next room, and he was *not* even guilty. I left the courtroom that day never to return, holding anger and bitterness close to me. I wanted nothing more to do with it. After all, I made the right decisions; I was on a path to change and, just like that, everything had taken leaps backwards. I didn't want anyone to feel sorry for me, and I didn't play the victim role, but the truth was, I felt so victimized and I was emotionally scared.

This chapter in my life almost drove me off the deep end. I cut off fourteen inches of my hair and dyed it red. I bought a gun. I cut off everybody and trusted no one. I was cruel, selfish; out to get what I could from men without any regard for their feelings.

I went to a rape crisis therapist for counseling, and that was helpful, but I needed something more. At times I felt like I needed an exorcism;

OK, not that bad, but close. I needed my guardian angel to step in and save me from what no one else could. I needed a lifeline. I needed to be **recharged** in some way; new energy needed to flow through me. I began to pray to God and ask for forgiveness and profess to him that I would make only the best decisions if he took away the hatred I had for Daniel. That is what was at the forefront of my mind; this incident had just sent me over the top.

Letting it Go

As time went on good intentions from men didn't matter. I allowed the rape to turn me into someone I didn't recognize in the mirror. I was mad at myself, the rapist, and everyone else, too. I didn't know **how** to get over it, but I desperately wanted to. I didn't want to be that mean, spiteful person. It was eating me up from the inside out. I was so bitter I could taste it.

Evelyn was a lady minister who I'd heard was anointed; she lived right across the street from my parents' house at that time. I had never gone to her church before, but had heard only good things about her. I called her up and told her what I had gone through and that I wanted—needed—for her to pray for me. She agreed to see me at her house and we set a date for me to come over that week.

When I arrived there were two other ladies there. She told me they would **all** be praying for me. I know it may sound strange, but I was down for anything that would make me feel better mentally about waking up in the morning. They asked me to lie on the floor of her living room on my left side. On of them was behind me in the spooning position, one at my head, and the other had her hand over my womb. My God, those women prayed for me so hard I literally threw up what resembled yolk or mucus. It was as if the bitterness and hate that was eating me from the inside had come out. I couldn't believe what had happened. It was the closest to God that I had ever felt at that time and is still one of my top three Lord-have-mercy-I-know-you're-real experiences of my life. I didn't hate the rapist any longer, and I moved on from that knowing that God was there for me when I truly was on the brink of self-destruction.

And just so I am painting the right picture…I wasn't marching around angry. For the most part I loved life. I enjoyed my freedom, family, and friends. I was intelligent and witty. I knew I would be successful and that I was "special" in some way. I did everything I set my mind to, no matter how small or big and no matter what stood in my way. But beneath the surface, these were my thoughts, my struggles, and my demons.

With that being said – my distrust for men up until that point didn't vanish in an instant like I'd hoped. As I got older, I constantly threw my "independent woman" badge up at every man I met for years after that. I spent much of my early to mid-twenties emotionally and spiritually lost, trying to find my way. Letting men know I didn't really need them, and that they were an option, and that if they were "real men," they could handle me and my nasty attitude. Had any song screaming independence been out then, I probably would have had it as my voice mail greeting and played it at the beginning of each date. It was that bad. I didn't want a man, but I wanted a man, needed one if I'm honest about it. But I couldn't show any sign of weakness or loss of control for fear of what they'd do to me. So I turned up the heat and turned on the intimidation factor.

CHAPTER
4

UNPLANNED PARENTHOOD

Parents can only give good advice or put them on the right paths, but
the final forming of a person's character lies in their own hands.

—ANNE FRANK

A few years after the rape I became pregnant by a guy I had been seeing for a couple of months. I already had baby Shania and she was only
two years old when I found out. *I'd gotten pregnant on purpose with Shania when
I turned eighteen. She was someone who would always be special to me.* The news of
a new baby possibly on the way wasn't a good time for me, and my initial thought was to abort. I contemplated it several times to the point of
making the appointment—then not showing up. I must have called and
rescheduled that same appointment five or six times before I made my
final decision.

During the time I found out I was pregnant I'd just met BJ, a *street phar-
macist* from Florida. I have to add, I wasn't raised in the ghetto or the hood,
I didn't know what government assistance was until my father retired from

the Military when I was in high school. Even with our household dysfunction, doing things outside of the law or associating with 'street folk' was not something I was accustomed too. With that being said, young people do stupid unexplainable things.

BJ was extremely handsome and kind to me and baby Shania. His demeanor was calm and he treated his <u>business</u> like a multi- million dollar corporation. My time with BJ wasn't a real relationship in the sense that we were in love, because we were not. We respected each other and treated our relationship more like a partnership. I like him, a lot and enjoyed his company. I knew what my role was and he played his part as well. There were no arguments or jealous fits; just nice times until it all when south on Valentines' Day in 1997. To make a long story short, I nearly got myself killed in a shoot out that evening. I knew right away that that wasn't the type of life I wanted for me, baby Shania or the new baby which I hadn't decided really what I wanted to do with. I knew I had to move, like asap! I needed a change, a big one. I was too good for that type of lifestyle. Yes, I said too good. Getting shot at was not my idea of success.

Before moving I had been researching adoption agencies. I relocated to Dallas just a month later to start my new life and leave the past where it was at. At that point I had to get serious about what I was going to do with the pregnancy. I was so torn over it. I didn't want to be like my cousins or my biological mother, Lynn, having a hand full (or more) children that I couldn't afford to feed or clothe. I didn't want to cheat my self, Shania or the new baby. I was much too afraid of the actual abortion procedure—so that was a no-go. I chose an adoption agency there. Once I was semi settled with a job and living with my aunt and uncle just outside of Dallas—I met with the attorney and began the search for a family for Baby J. At this point I had told the father that I was expecting and his response was "why are you telling me?" So I knew not to expect any help or support from him.

Though I was adopted as an infant I thought my mother, Mary, would have been more accepting of my choice to 'adopt out' the baby—she wasn't. No one wanted me to do it. People always put in their two cents but aren't there to help you feed, clothe and raise the child. *Black people don't do that, they keep their babies!* I heard that more than I needed too. I always thought that was strange especially since it was no secret that I'm black and adopted.

I also saw all much of my family on welfare and living in public housing too. That wasn't a life I was accustomed to or wanted for myself or my children at any point. And for those of you who will say, there's nothing wrong with living in public housing—I agree but not for generations! So I ignored everyone and did exactly what I thought was best for Baby J.

I wanted an Open Adoption. I needed to know that Baby J was developing well and what she looked like through the years. So after looking at numerous profiles I found a family that wanted what I wanted—and so we began the process. I always felt good about the decision to adopt out but it hurt like hell. I wanted to be pregnant for ever. I never wanted to have her. I wanted to keep her with me. Giving birth would mean my time with Baby J was over...

Picking parents for your child is like picking a father. Choose wisely and carefully. This decision helped me understand it was the same thing. The same type of decision; and had I taken it more seriously I wouldn't have gotten pregnant in the first place—but it was much to late for that type of thinking.

After many visits to the doctor and appointments with the chosen parents, Baby J was about to be due—man. My doctor was the best; I was off work for several months prior to giving birth to her. I remember locking myself in my room and grieving the entire time Princess Diana's funeral aired. It was the first week of September 1997—Baby J was due just a couple weeks after that. I never paid much attention to the Royal Family or any other world news, but the timing was disturbingly perfect. I mourned Princess Di and Baby J at the same time. And because my labor was being induced I knew just how many days I had—and it wasn't enough.

The day I went in to be induced, I just remember the gut wrenching feeling of leaving the hospital without her. I allowed her chosen parents to be in the room during delivery. I made the most out of my days in the hospital. Holding and kissing her, loving on her, changing her diapers and feeding her. I was so thankful that we were able to spend this time together. Though she would never remember it, that day will always be Mother's Day to me. It would **have** to last....I was happy for her 'parents' but sad for me. I wanted her, I always wanted her—but I was lost and didn't know which way was up or down. So I made the best choice at the time. Her parent gave me a beautiful silver bracelet with the affirmation *"Forever Grateful"* engraved inside. It's the only real piece of jewelry I owned for nearly fifteen years. The only thing that gave me peace was the fact that I hoped we'd be reunited when she turns 18. I always hoped she would want to know who I was—I have always kept in touch and I hope she knows how much I love her. It's 2011; she'll be 14 this year, 4 years to go and counting.

Her biological father and I have maintained a friendship throughout the years. He regrets his comments about the pregnancy and asks about her whenever we speak.

PART TWO

Life's a Journey

CHAPTER
5

THE INTIMIDATION FACTOR
WHO'S REALLY AFRAID OF WHO

Fear is the main source of superstition, and one of the main
sources of cruelty. To conquer fear is the beginning of wisdom.

– BERTRAND RUSSELL

Generally speaking, the type of man you want is one who is **not** intimidated by you, me, or any woman, including those who proclaim to be
independent. Intimidation implies fear—and most men aren't fearful of
anything. Not you, your career, your education, or your successes. The
notion that they are is a falsehood proliferated by the media, online bloggers, independent women gone bad and angry men. I think the truth is
women are intimidated by men and what they *might* do to us. Intimidated
by our past hurts and our imaginations. And while men want to "be the
man" and feel needed and useful, most men want a woman who is self-
sufficient—who has the ability to handle her own affairs and take care of
herself, both desirable qualities. But for every one of the more desirable-
type women, there are women out there that intentionally threaten men by
their actions because they have been hurt. There are many women hiding

behind promiscuity, physically and verbally abusive relationships, and fear; those things are controlling their true womanhood. What you see isn't the real them, isn't the real you because you haven't been the real you—you don't even know who she is.

With that being said, of course it's not that simple or easily explained, but I'll do my best. From my perspective, there are two sides of the intimidation factor. I'll go through each one separately.

1) Women's intention to intimidate men to remain in control out of fear; acting the part
2) Types of men who are dealing with and who *would be* intimidated by a woman, and whether or not it's really intimidation.

"Acting" the Part

Why would I or any woman intentionally try to intimidate a man? Aren't we attracted to strong, assertive men? Men who want to take charge of situations so we don't have to? The short answer is yes. But let's get down to the truth about this.

I always wanted a man who wasn't afraid to tell me no or take control of the reins. I wanted a man who wasn't afraid of me and my attitude. I seriously believed that if a man stuck around after my mistreatment or being talked "crazy" to, then he was potentially strong enough to "handle me," as I mentioned earlier. If he can deal with me at my worst, he can have me at my best, I'd say. I wanted **that** type of man. But truthfully I would never let it happen, because I was too guarded. I'd be kicking and screaming all the way. There was no way in hell I would let a man take charge of any decisions in my life when it came to a relationship. I carried my independent woman persona daily, acting as if it gave me permission to be a bitch because of what I had experienced in the past. I turned up the intimidation factor in order to protect my heart, testing men, thus keeping them at a safe distance.

I constantly felt the need to prove just how independent I was. And, in doing so, I emasculated or attempted to emasculate every man I came in contact with—then used the "well, he's just intimated by me" line as a fallback for my own issues. But really, I was sabotaging any hopes of a relationship out of fear. Anytime I had the chance to convey an autonomous attitude, I did. It became second nature to me—a justification to be aggressive or snappy any time my abilities were tested or questioned. Immediately I was on the defensive with men, which in turn taught me how to be manipulative in an attempt to intimidate them into understanding just how little I truly needed them in my life.

My need to protect myself always made me feel as if they were inferior, sending my brain murky messages that I was, in fact, superior. I can admit that for years I added fuel to the negative stigma associated with the term "independent woman." And because that was my mind-set, subconsciously I acted it out and played the part. Which was so ass backwards because I really **wanted** deeply to trust a man to be "the man." But the fear of what could go wrong was too real for me—so I prevented it at all costs. If that meant acting the part of Miss Too Damn Independent, then that's what I did. I couldn't let it go—nothing in me would allow that type of release; the type of trust needed to allow that to occur wasn't a part of who I was at the time. I wish I could say I didn't know I was doing it, but I did. I only turned on the intimidation factor when I felt I had to.

I must confess…

When I was in my early twenties, I don't believe I thought men were intimidated by my drive and self-determination, but I wanted them to be. I knew there was an independent woman inside of me, but the persona I put on at times was a negative one. I hoped that it would protect me in advance—an effort to preempt any hurt they might cause me. It was all for show. So that way, if something didn't work out, it was easier for me to blame it on the man. I never looked into my own backyard. I wasn't ready for that type of self-inventory just yet.

I moved to Dallas in 1997 and eventually settled into a one-bedroom apartment with Shania. I worked full time and enjoyed my single life and the elements of the new city. I loved it there!

Ryan. He and I dated briefly back in high school. He was the guy my mother forbade me to see. It was a simple crush; we had a puppy love connection and had only kissed once. It was very innocent and sweet. After I had been in Dallas for about a year, we'd reconnected through a mutual friend. At this point, it had been about eight years since we'd heard from or seen each other. So this reconnection was my chance to see "what would happen if", now that we were adults. I was always optimistic about love; I wanted it to be real and true. I always wanted to give it a chance—even if it hurt.

That first phone call we talked for three or four hours into the night. He was familiar and comforting. He knew me before I was raped, before Doc—a period of time when my innocence was somewhat intact. It was like a clean slate for me.

He ended that first call with, "I'll see you in the morning." And just like that, the next morning he was on his way from Clarksville, Tennessee, to Dallas to spend the weekend with Shania and me. I was thoroughly impressed with that. I mean, it was just the next day and we hadn't seen each other since we were teenagers.

I couldn't sleep much that night in anticipation of seeing him again. As the sun arose, the thought of being reunited with him in just a few hours was becoming more a reality by the minute. After some preparation and primping, I headed over to a nearby shopping center to await his arrival. I recall sitting in my 1996 green Ford Escort in front of Burger King, waiting anxiously. The timing was perfect; as he drove up I was all smiles. Standing in front of my face after all that time, cute as ever, was Ryan, and looking the same (maybe a little thinner) since high school. Took me right back to being a hormonal, pimply faced fifteen-year-old again. We had a long, "I'm so glad to see you" embrace and stood there in the parking lot in disbelief, smiling, blushing, and acting like teenagers again for several minutes before we headed to my apartment. It was an endearing moment. Like the one in the movies when two lovers are running in slow motion through the meadows towards each other—all you see are butterflies and flowers, and all you hear is elevator music.

It was a great weekend. I introduced him to my Bianca and Sonya, we went out, and did a few touristy things, then back to Tennessee he went on Sunday night, just in time for work on Monday morning. Several phone calls and a couple of weeks later, Ryan relocated to Dallas and moved in with me. I was twenty-two at the time, and it didn't occur to me that if a man can pick up, leave everything he knows and loves, and move 650 miles away at the drop of a dime, his life can't be all that stable! But I wasn't thinking that far ahead—I was young and dumb and thought he must really be into me to do something so drastic. This must be meant to be, right? A long-lost love…I sure hoped so.

Ryan was what I called "cute," with a vanilla cocoa complexion and the brightest smile. Although he didn't think he was very attractive and had some self-esteem issues, he was very sweet. I'd later find out that he had some other issues that had nothing to do with me. He hadn't seen his parents or brother in seven years or so at that point. He also had a son that he was barely permitted to see by the ignorant women he was with years before me. He was a great father and loved his son more than I can explain, but the idea that he couldn't see him was eating him at the core. We were truly an emotional mess—but even with that, we were willing to work through it and give it a shot. I was able to suppress my issues much better than he was. I was too busy being successful; Ryan was all over the place. We were kind of a mess individually—trying to have a relationship.

Ryan found a temp job fairly quickly—he was a blue-collar worker, not a bum at all—he just didn't make a lot of money. But our income combined made it OK, and I liked him, a lot. I was working a regular job in legalization but had been introduced to network marketing by a good friend of mine, Emmett. So I'd begun associating myself with people on a level at which I could see myself in the near future. It was a more professional world that I fit into quite nicely. I enjoyed connecting with new people, and the hype of network marketing motivated me to want success. Ryan, on the other hand, never felt comfortable in that environment. It was like when you go to a company function and you work the room introducing your date to your colleagues, and he is just out of place no matter what he tries to do. It just wasn't his cup of tea; he didn't fit in and I knew it. I still made every attempt to stroke his ego and validate him in ways I thought he needed so he'd be comfortable, but it wasn't enough. It wasn't about me—there was something in him.

Even with those differences, we had a good time together, he was a good father figure for my daughter, and we were OK. He was a hard worker and happily paid his share of the bills. About nine months or so into it, his insecurities were overshadowing our relationship. I didn't know how to deal with him because I was still figuring myself out, finding my place—who is Aprille Franks? He claimed I was cheating with my best male friend, which was something he'd conjured up in his mind. My friend Emmett is still my friend today and we've never even kissed. We're like family. Never was I unfaithful to him—not even when I could have been. I was committed to our relationship. And, let the truth be told, I believe Ryan slept with one of my "friends," and if he didn't, he flirted with the idea of it. But I suppressed that thought. As time went on, we ended up pregnant—which I had mixed emotions about, but was still planning to have the baby and be with him. His insecurities and emotional issues played into the notion that the baby wasn't his. Unfreakinbelievable. I made sure he knew he was loved and appreciated. But again, it wasn't enough. There were too many things eating at him that I couldn't fix, and it wasn't my place to either.

Early one morning I'd fallen asleep in the living room, and was awakened by him walking out of the front door headed to work. It was about 4 a.m., a normal day like any other. I didn't have to be at work for another couple of hours so I just turned over and drifted back to sleep. Eventually I got up, showered, dropped Shania off at day care, then headed to work. Ryan normally called me on his lunch break, but not that day. That day was different. He worked in a plant, so I figured he'd gotten busy and couldn't call me, so I blew it off. But after a while I grew concerned, so I called his job and, to my surprise, he *hadn't* been to work that day. I didn't want to believe he'd lied to me, but if it looks like a duck.... Truth is I didn't know what to think. I didn't know where he was or could have been. Neither of us had a cell phone at that time, so I had to wait for him to call me at work or home later that evening. The call never came. After work I rushed home hoping he'd be there, but he wasn't.

And like most women, before we go off the deep end, we think the worst—something may have happened, is he OK, did he get in an accident—and nine times out ten, they are just being men, doing whatever the hell they want to do without consideration of our distress.

As I began to get into my normal just-coming-home routine, I began to notice little things were out of place—missing. I checked around our apartment and noticed his *shit* was missing—and that he had actually moved out in the middle of the night. My seeing him leave for "work" was him leaving me. But where was he? Who knew? OK, true distress began to set in as I was storming through my apartment looking for signs that this man didn't *really* just move out and didn't say anything to me! We didn't have an argument or a "honey, we need to talk" moment, so I was totally dumbfounded. But there was <u>nothing</u> I could do. I had no way to get in touch with him, so I just waited. For days, I waited and waited for a call, but nothing. I was in disbelief. What kind of man moves out of the house while you're sleeping, after nearly a year of being together, and says nothing? Talk about disappearing acts! None of my girlfriends could believe it and neither could I. Everyone loved him...including my daughter and me. There were no signs that he was moving out, not even in my 20/20 hindsight!

A week or so later he called me at work, and proceeded to tell me that he had actually moved back to Nashville and wasn't coming back. Yep. He just packed his bags and moved in a split second, just the way he came. No good-byes to me, Shania, and never mind the pregnancy. He just did the best thing for him. He admitted he had things he needed to deal with, but damn—can you give a girl some notice? I was <u>in the way</u> of him dealing with that. And for him, he was always in my territory, which he felt like he had to compete with. For me, it was *our* territory. I believe that in his mind, he couldn't live up to what he thought I was doing…and I wasn't even doing that much in my mind, but my *potential* was threating to him. He had some issues and things to work out that had nothing to do with me. I don't know if he was intimidated, and I hate to even use the word… but sometimes it is what it is. I can't make it sound good because of a man's ego or lack thereof. Whichever the case, I was in love and still wanted to be with him. Yep, even after him leaving me high and dry.

About two weeks later in the middle of the night, to make matters worse, I began to cramp and bleed vaginally. I called my friend Emmett to come and get Shania, then called 911to come and get me. They transported me to the emergency room as Emmett followed. I got to the emergency room and they put me in a room immediately, I was in such pain. Emmett, his two toddlers, and Shania were standing in the doorway. I stood up and walked towards them to hug Shania, and before I could get there, the fetus fell out of me and onto the floor. I heard it splat. I can't find a word in the English dictionary to explain how I felt in that moment. I was beyond devastated as I stood there like a statue, hoping what I thought had just happened didn't really just happen. But it did. The nurses ran to my aid and Emmett stood there in shock for a moment before he took the kids away. I had miscarried, and Ryan wasn't even there to tell me it would be all right, to hold my hand, nothing. Bastard. And not that we needed a baby at that time or things were perfect between us, but it would have been all right. God had another plan, I guess.

Over the course of the next few weeks, Ryan and I attempted to work it out, and I took my silly ass to Nashville a couple of months later. Left my job I had had since I moved to Dallas in 1997, left everything behind. I knew I had some things to work through as well, but I was naïve in thinking he could be something different, because I loved him. I wanted to believe that he could be the type of man I wanted/needed him to be. I didn't understand that he just wasn't the type of man I needed. There was nothing to be done; he would never be for me and we would have never worked. But I had to learn the hard way.

Still not over the Dallas incident, there I was, in Nashville, Tennessee, of all places. We shared an apartment and both of us worked full time. But for whatever reason, we only had one key to our apartment. One evening Ryan was headed out somewhere and I wanted him to leave the key. The lock was one of those double-sided keyed locks—you needed a key on both sides to get in or out. For whatever reason he didn't want to leave the key with me. My concern was if something happened we (Shania and I) would be trapped in the apartment—and **then** I felt controlled. The idea of him thinking he could lock me the apartment on the second floor just sent me over top. We began arguing, and I remember breaking his cell phone, then he threw mine in the pool just off the balcony. It was immature and petty. But all I could think was he *isn't* going anywhere with those keys. So like a deranged young girl, I threw a jack through the windshield of his car. I really couldn't think at that point. I only saw red and my past flashing before me. Being controlled or feeling controlled was not something I was able to deal with. I always had to have the upper hand. If I didn't, I could or would be hurt. My messing with his car, of course, just pissed him off, and now whatever plans he had planned were ruined.

After about an hour of back-and-forth arguing, I just needed him to give me some space; but he wouldn't. So I ran to the kitchen and grabbed a knife and told him to *please* leave me alone. But he wouldn't; he pushed, pushed and pushed me until I couldn't take it anymore. I still can't believe I picked up that knife, but I did, and I ultimately ended up cutting him as he grabbed for it and caught the serrated blade. The night ended with me dropping him off at the ER. I was so mean about it too; I can only shake my head today. I left him in the next couple of days.

The truth was, being with Ryan showed me you can have no intention of being intimidating and still be perceived that way by the other person. But on the flip side, my need to not feel intimidated and not to be controlled ultimately controlled me. I realized that I needed to work on myself in a major way. Following him around the country, being accused of things I wasn't doing, knowing he possibly cheated with a "friend," being abandoned with a pregnancy—it boiled down to my self-worth and self-esteem. Sure, I knew he had some things to deal with, but I knowingly accepted him with those issues. I had to be honest with myself, in that every man I made the decision to be with may not have been the best choice for me. Many decisions I made were based on how I felt, not necessarily what was best for me. And before I could focus on the type of man that was best for me, I had to acknowledge I still had some work to do.

Intimidation Part II—who are you dealing with

The second part of the intimidation factor is the types of men spend our time with—because we shouldn't be with them anyway. The signs are all there, but we choose to ignore them because we've become emotionally attached in some way. Then we claim we have high standards and use that as an excuse as to why the last twenty dates were a failure or the past four relationships didn't work out, when in actuality we are swimming in the wrong pond or fishing where we shouldn't be. Then we wonder why it doesn't work out with "Mikey" or why he continues to disappoint us, instead of asking ourselves why we keep letting him.

Men prove to us time and time again their level of manhood with their actions and inactions. They will categorize themselves, and it's up to us to pay attention when they do—and not get in the way and attempt to do it for them. Know what you want and recognize when it wants you back. Just as women go through stages, men go through various stages of manhood before they settle into what works for them. Oftentimes we try to make a man fit into our idea of what he should or could be when it's not in his make-up to do so, or when he's simply not ready to be the type of man you need, when you need it.

Through my dating experiences, I've identified four types of men as they relate to independent women. There is no science to this; just my own observations and experiences. Here they are:

Rock

Baby Boy

Commando

Honey

1) Rock

This man is a well-rounded blue- or white-collar worker. You don't intimidate him in the least bit. He wants to be the breadwinner and take care of the family. He respects the woman in his life and will give her everything she wants and needs within his means. He simply prefers a more traditional relationship style, and, in his mind, a man should be the head of the house and be the one taking care of you and his family. Your independent womanhood doesn't work with his ego. In a restaurant, Rock is most likely to sit facing the entrance as to protect you should someone approach you from behind. He is a protector.

Don't mistake his desire to take charge of his family to equal intimidation of you. And unless he says "you intimidate me," don't assume so, just to make yourself feel better. Don't think he's intimidated by you—even with all the wonderful things about you that *you think* makes you a good catch. We are not all things to everybody, no matter how good a woman we think we are. Good and real are matters of perception, which may not be the truth in reality. He may never admit it to you that your independent womanhood wasn't his preference; the relationship either "just didn't work out" or "you're a sidepiece" or you're better off as "friends." This man will end up with a woman you deem "lower" in standards. Don't wonder why; it's simple: she fit into his mold.

2) Baby Boy

He's not there yet (and may never be when you want him to be). This man admires what you have accomplished with the challenges you've faced but holds some resentment because of your success. While he *is* a hard worker and has potential, he has a way to go. This man may have felt as though he wasn't good enough to be with you at times. And by observing you, he's recognized there are some areas in his own life that he needs to improve upon or things he should have accomplished by this stage of the game. Men are held to a higher standard, and you've surpassed him already. This may also make him think that he is less than a man because he knows he could be doing as well as you, if not better than you. While his doing better than you may not be as important to you, he's still a man. You are too many steps ahead of the race for him to catch up or pass you, so he quits and does one of two things: 1) he gets himself together for the next women in line, taking all the things you said into action, or 2) he finds a woman on the level you were on about five years ago. This gives him a chance. He can now ride the wave; she can look up to him. They can achieve milestones together.

> This is one of those situations when you can't understand why your ex is suddenly dating a woman in school or who makes less money than you. It's not about status quo. It's about his needs and whether they are being met in the way he needs.

3) Commando

Commando is drawn to you and wants you. He's attracted to your abilities alone and is intrigued by what you could bring to a relationship. He himself is accomplished, self-assured, responsible, and finds you more refreshing than challenging. The fact that you are of like minds is a turn-on for him. He is looking for a woman who can accept his position and has her own thoughts, ideas, and goals not totally dependent upon him. He wants a worldly woman who can carry on an intelligent conversation and respect him equally. This couple is a power couple. This man enjoys doing things for you that put a smile on your face—not because he has to, or because you need him to, but because he genuinely wants to. Intimidation? There's no such thing.

4) Honey

He's smooth, charismatic, and attractive to you. He loves independent women because they are a meal ticket. He *can* hold down a 9-to-5 job, but his main position is filling in the nonfinancial gaps in your life. To make you feel good about yourself because you don't. He is simply living off of your ignorance, love, and desperation. He'll entertain you as long as you allow him to. He's not emotionally attached to you but may enjoy your company. You're a commodity which can be replaced if someone better comes along. He doesn't have his "stuff" together and he's not even thinking about his future—only yours and how he can benefit. You keep him around because he boosts your ego in some fashion and the sex is usually explosive. He's a dead end. He needs a mother figure, a sugar momma, not a woman.

At the end of the day the intimidation factor goes both ways, but it's all in the power of the woman. Conquering the fear and self defeating behavior is apart of this process. When we neglect our true needs, we end up with a Honey when we really want and need a Rock. The power lies within us. We guide more of the relationship dynamic than we think. We need to get to know ourselves better, know what we want and what we will and won't accept.

CHAPTER
6

GIRLFRIENDS
BREAKING UP IS HARD TO DO

Nothing but heaven itself is better than a friend who is really a friend.

—PLAUTUS

The time I spent in Dallas was a defining point in my life; it's where I began to think bigger about everything. I began to see the type of life I could have professionally and I ran with it. It's also where I learned even more about myself, parenting, men and friendships. It's where I became close with two very special women; Sonya and Bianca. We all worked together. All of our children were the same age give or take a year or two. At that time they were just toddlers. Not only were the relationships in my life with men impactful—so were the relationships I developed with my Girlfriends. I never trusted anyone with my life and well being like I trusted these ladies. Sonya and Bianca met prior to me relocating to Dallas—so I was the newest addition making the duo a trio.

Sonya was a few years older than Bianca and I. Bianca was the youngest of the group. All of us had very different stories and backgrounds.

Sonya was from a small town with the influence of both parents in her life—great parents might I add. She had the 'American dream' life plan. College, then marriage, two children back to back so they'd grow up together, hopefully a boy and a girl, while working her way up in the corporate world. I respected her and her strong family unit.

Bianca was also married with a daughter. Her married life was very different from Sonya's at first. She lived her married life mostly in single mode. There issues with Bianca and her husband were toxic. They'd been together since they were very young and kinda stuck to what they knew no matter how bad or ugly it got—the dysfunction worked for them in some twisted way. She was from Dallas and as a young teenager had to step up and raise her little brother because her mother was a drug addict. Bianca was forced to be responsible and survive on her own at an early age. She and I were similar in that failure was really not an option. Bianca was the first homeowner among us. We were proud of her, she was a really hard worker.

The three of us were as close as girlfriends could be. We didn't make a lot of money during the late 1990's but we sure had a ball together. We all certainly made the most of what we had. Each of us had our own relationships within the group and that worked well. We balanced each other out—it was an awesome dynamic.

Living in Dallas during this era in my early twenties life was on a natural high! There was always something to do and an array of men to keep us entertained. We had some of the best times and there were many instances when we were a life line for one another during hard times. Through our personal growth, successes, unfaithful husbands, car repossessions and the scheming games we played with men —we were always there for each other. We were a unit and honestly, I couldn't imagine my life at that time without them and their children. We were a family even through our differences—well, to a point.

As time went on Sonya and I had a couple of run ins. She didn't really have them with me, I had them with her. There were times when I felt as though she was trying to handle me (and others) when it was convenient for her or when she wanted or needed something – and I didn't like that in the least bit. She was one of those people you'd call and she'd call you back—eventually! You'd have to track her down at times. Oh, but please know that you needed to be available when she wanted or needed you. For about six months we didn't really talk because I felt as though she didn't respect my time but expected everyone to respect hers. But eventually as friends do, we talked it out, made up and got over it but it taught me a valuable lesson about people; no matter how important people are to you in *your* life know that you may *not* be as important to them. Their life is about them and their needs, first. I also learned to accept people for who they are—just like family. You accept them and don't sweat the small stuff. She wasn't changing so I had to either accept her or not. So our friendship continued as it always had.

A couple years after she was married and had her two children, her plan began to fall apart when she discovered her husband was cheating on her. I remember it like it clearly. We were all at work that day and Sonya was devastated. She didn't deserve it, not that anyone does, but she really was a model wife. She struggled with staying in the marriage for a while, but soon she was in single mode as Bianca was. Because of her strong family unit, Sonya was going to be okay no matter what but that situation did change her. Bianca and I were there for her as much as we could be.

Over the years Sonya and I periodically kept in contact. We were more off than on and I've seen her a few times over the years. We've since grown apart—and I'm okay with that, it happens. She was a good friend when I needed her to be and hopefully she can say the same about me today.

I bring up the girlfriends in my life because we need them like they need us. We need them to be honest with us and there for us when something monumental or petty occurs in our lives. They help to keep us level—mostly. But sometimes we can become too close and begin to depend on them or them on us beyond the friendship realm. Many times our girlfriends are our "metaphoric men"—it doesn't matter if you're married or single. We date them, cry with them, laugh with them, grow with them, travel with them and break up with them too.

When I made the decision to leave Ryan in Tennessee, Bianca was one of the first calls I made. At that time she wasn't working so we decided to be roommates in order to help each other out. The timing was perfect because her husband had just recently moved out of the house. I packed my bags, loaded the moving truck and back to Dallas I went. Because I'd let my job go after being there for 4 years to follow Ryan—finding new employment was my main priority. I always worked and had a job and found one almost immediately upon my arrival to Dallas. At the time Bianca was going to school and she had the only car. I swear it was like a marriage. She'd take me to work, and pick me up—we'd cook and make sure the kids had what they needed and so on. We did everything but have sex together. If one had, the other had. I didn't have the type of closeness with my own family growing up so these women *were* my family. When that's apart of your story you either value your friends like family or don't have many friends. I valued mine.

But when you're dealing with your own life's journey, your past and your present uncertainties—it's hard to be the best friend you can be. Not only is it difficult, but the truth is it's not a priority!

After a few months of me being back in Dallas and sharing the house with Bianca, she began to get 'friendly' with her husband again. I had no respect for him because of the way he treated her and I just thought he was a loser—we **all** knew she could do better. He couldn't provide for her in the way she needed and he was abusive. As her friend I was tired of seeing her go through the mess with him and she seriously deserved better. Anyhow, she loved him and as her friend, I had to accept it so I held my tongue for years but I would journal about them and everything else going on in my life. Her husband was jealous of the closeness Bianca and I had. She and I knew we could trust each other and that we were a *constant*—the men came and went.

So it's December 2001 and Bianca drops me off at work like any other day. I work until about ten o'clock that evening. She picks me up and begins talking, within about five minutes tells me that she wants me to move out. I remember exactly what I said that evening, "okay." I knew what it was about and I wasn't about talking women out of doing crazy shit because of the men in their lives—I'd been there and done that with my cousin Roxy back in my teens. I asked her when did she want me to move and she said "tonight." This really hurt because just the day before I'd given her my entire check ($432 to be exact) and had $10 left to my name, no car and now, no place to live. We didn't argue about it—or have any ill words. When we arrived at her house she'd already packed up all of my things. That is what pissed me off to no end. I wasn't mad about moving out; I knew how women worked when it came to low self worth and men. After all, I was one of *those* women. I was hurt by *the way* she chose to do it.

I had a bed there and some other things too large and heavy to carry so I asked her could we stay until the next morning and she knew we had no where to go—but she said "No" anyway. I remember one of the last things she said to me as I was standing there was, "I hope you get what you deserve!" I didn't even know where that came from but was thinking *"I hope you do too....you evil b*!"* I transferred everything I could into a black duffle bag, grabbed Shania by her 4 year old hand—and out the front door in the cold darkness we went. We just walked and walked.

> I think its amazing how people think they have any authority over your life or any say as to how you will progress or digress. As if they are God and have some power over you, when in actuality they have <u>nothing</u> but their own demons to fight.

We stopped at a nearby payphone and the first call I made was to my mother. I told her what happened and that I needed to come home— back to Mobile, Alabama. Even though we had our bouts growing up, I could and still can—go back home anytime. That was a sad phone call, I just cried like a baby. The next call I made was to Sonya. I told her what happened and she couldn't believe it. She couldn't fathom Bianca just putting my daughter and I out and was shocked that we didn't have some big blow up—but we didn't. Bianca did what was best for her—and her husband.

The last call I made was to KD, I'll talk more about him in the next Chapter: A Desperate Kind of Love.

Sonya lived about forty-five minutes away in Lewisville, Texas and picked us up as we were walking along Garland Road and we crashed at her house for the night. Tears and talking, then more tears and even more talking ensued that night. Sonya loaned me the money for our bus tickets and just like that we were to leave Dallas at one o'clock that next day. Your life can change in an instant. I was hurt by Bianca's actions but I didn't have time to deal with it or think about the real reason behind it. I had to figure out my situation and move on, quickly.

The next morning was pretty emotional. My first stop was to go and see KD—we met him in the parking lot of the printing company he worked for at the time. Talk about, boohoo sobbing. I'll never forget his face when I stepped out of the car—we were all an emotional mess. Sonya was shedding tears in her car as well. Sure I had planned to leave Dallas and go back to Mobile within a couple of months anyway but that was supposed to be a happy occasion, with a going away party and parting gifts! I sat in the car with KD and just cried. I wasn't ready to leave Dallas, my friends or him. We talked and talked. He handed me some cash for the trip and we said our "I love you's" then off we went on our separate ways.

It was a peaceful eighteen hour bus ride back to Mobile that day. I remember getting to my parents house and sitting in the living room on the sofa thinking about my life. Thinking about what I was going to do with it and what did I truly want it to look like? Thinking about the time I'd wasted and how I could fix it. Sure, I was sad and honestly heartbroken that my friend, my sister, my confidante would put my daughter and I out in the middle of the night. I couldn't dwell in it for long. About a month after being back at my parent's house I wrote her a letter, letting her know that I'd forgiven her and that Shania and I were just fine. I also sent her an envelope to send back my *"Forever Grateful"* bracelet but to no avail. I don't really blame Bianca; she did what was best for her at the time. It wasn't about me—I was just caught up in it.

About four years later Shania and I took a two week vacation to Dallas. It was Christmas 2005. I was dating Nick in St. Louis at the time (I'll get to him soon enough). I made the decision to go see Bianca while I was there. I had two reasons for this. The first was I wanted her to 'see' that I'd gotten exactly what I deserved. Happiness and I was successful in my career in property management. The second reason was to get my *"Forever Grateful"* bracelet I'd left behind by mistake the last time we saw each other.

I knocked on the door and she was home. "Who is it?" she yelled. "It's Aprille." She screamed, "Aprille who?!" as she was opening the door. I am sure she was shocked to see me because I didn't call because I didn't have a number —I just showed up out of the blue after all those years. We talked for a couple of hours and she had several of my things in a little box that were important to me. That let me know that maybe she *was* a friend when *she **was** a friend*. She could have thrown my belongings away but she didn't. I don't think either of us was as authentic as we could have been during that visit. I know my intentions were not 100% sincere and because I know her, neither was hers.

Surprisingly, last summer (July 2010) I saw Bianca at our mutual friend, Corey Wilson's birthday soiree in Dallas. We talked about it after a couple of drinks. When I asked her why she put us out her response was "I didn't know what else to do". I didn't expect to be touched by it in the least because I hadn't thought twice about it or her in recent years but seeing her brought up all of those memories I'd grown to expect men to treat women with disregard but to my surprise my deepest hurt came from a "friend". She hurt me more than any man ever had—because I could have never anticipated being disregarded like trash by any friend of mine much less, Bianca.

I don't have anything negative to say about Bianca but I don't have anything more to say either. She was a seasonal friend in my life and as I was in hers. I have grown to appreciate the life lessons our friendship has taught me and that's where I am with that. Nothing more, nothing less.

Let me add that I was not always the perfect friend to all of my friends but I was to her. Like anything, becoming a good friend is something we grown into.

CHAPTER
7

A DESPERATE KIND OF LOVE
HER HUSBAND, MY HEART

Desperation is like stealing from the Mafia:
you stand a good chance of attracting the wrong attention.

—DOUGLAS HORTON

No one sets out to fall in love in a way that you totally lose yourself, but it happens. I have never really thought of myself as being the desperate chick but there were definitely times when I acted out of desperation. The men and availability of men in my life were always abundant, some were amazing and others not so much, but abundant nonetheless. Even with that being true, fear had been a driving force in many of my decisions—all in the name of protecting myself or controlling a situation. Sometimes, many times, it was easier to do the wrong thing in the name of love because I didn't know who I was and was too busy to find out. Grab a corner and let's go back to nineteen ninety-eight, in Dallas for a while.

I must confess...

Talk about big laughs and good times with sister friends. Like I said, the kind of friends that *should* last forever, the kind of friends that you'd call in the middle of the night for advice, to keep your kids for a week while you stress out about nothing, the kind of friends that would tell you just how fat you look in that dress.

I'll never forget January 1998, celebrating Sonya's, birthday. Bianca, Sonya and I loved the Filling Station on Park Avenue. They served drinks with a two drink—maximum limit with fire blazing from the rim of the glass. As were sitting there she saw an old college flame, Eric. She told us about him in the seven seconds before he made it to our table. She gave us the whole "he was the one in college" rundown. I thought to myself, *"Forget about him, who's the fine guy with him?"* Tall, six foot one, 210 pounds, honey-complexioned man with the black trench coat! We were sitting in a half-moon booth and I was on the end.

"Oh my God! How are you?!" Eric said to Sonya.

"Great. It's my birthday; me and my girls are out celebrating!"

"Happy birthday," interrupted the Honey. "Oh, my fault, this is my boy KD!" Eric said.

Now, what I was sitting there thinking was simply—I want him just based on looks alone. He was mouthwatering fine...the kind of man you see and immediately your mind begins to take you down a hot, steamy, raunchy road. I knew nothing about this man, no last name, phone number, relationship status, five-year plan, nothing! But was something encapsulating about him that just drew me in. His smile, his bowed legs, his pecks, those arms.....

"Heeey, KD," we all sang in unison, like schoolgirls.

While Sonya was reminiscing with Eric and chatting with the other girls, KD and I were having a sideline conversation as we basically undressed each other at the table. Totally inappropriate, but appropriate for what I was thinking. We were all single people, no harm there, just a little harmless flirting.

"So where are you guys coming from?" I asked.

"We just finished a Sebastian photo shoot." KD said arrogantly.

A little arrogance is slightly attractive on the right man. I'm not easily impressed and besides I like to have to upper hand. Never the fan, never the groupie. I wanted a man to go crazy over **me**. I wanted to prove I could be on top. No pun intended.

"Oh, ok that's cool," I replied nonchalantly.

I could tell this man was used to women falling at his feet and tripping over each word that rolled off of his tongue and out of his mouth. Hmph, he'd never get that kind of satisfaction from me. A little more small talk ensued, then KD and I exchanged numbers and off they went.

A week or so later, it was work as usual, a day like any other. Phones ringing, faxes falling on the floor, and the Audit Department was basically running itself. My second line rang and I answered like normal. It was him, it was KD. *I knew he'd call.*

"May I speak to April?" he said.

"This is she, who's speaking?"

"KD. Hey girl, what's going on with you?"

"I'm pretty good, just working. What's up?" I said.

"You."

STOP. I hate it when a man says that. You don't even know me or anything about me! Translation—what that means is, "I'll screw you if you let me, **that's** what's up."

"Oh, OK, me huh?!" I said.

He then went on to tell me a little more about himself but not before he tells me he's married and that his wife was the most important thing to him and how nothing or no one comes before her.

Bull. The fact that he said that to me lets me know two things. One, she isn't that important; he just wanted me to think she was so I'd stay in my place or whatever category he put me in. Then, secondly, what's truly important is whatever we do past this point is none of his wife's business. His family isn't most important; what *he* wants is.

Surprisingly, there wasn't a moment of clarity—or morality, for that matter—in me that contemplated *not* meeting him. I never even thought about his wife. All I could think was, "How he dare think that he is in control of this situation because he is married?" That was my issue; I couldn't let a man think he was in control. It was a game, he wanted to play, and I was in. Checkmate. We planned to meet that next weekend.

I headed over to the address he gave me, referred to by him and his friends as the "honeycomb hideout." It was really his aunt's place. It was a hump stop away from the wives.

I remember driving through the gate, getting out of my car, walking along a winding sidewalk and up a flight of stairs. I was getting antsy with the anticipation of seeing him again. To prove I had the sexual upper hand, I prided myself on being a sexual goddess in the bedroom. And I knew he'd like it, then love it, then want more of it. The fact that he was married didn't come into play for me at that point. I was just proving a moot point.

Knock, knock. He answers the door, I walk in, and the mood is set. Soft music, dim lights, and cocktails. I don't remember talking about much, a little chitchat that leads us to an unspoken attraction between us. KD delivered the most passionate kisses I'd experienced. Hard, wet tongue; suck your bottom lip, hands around your neck kind of kissing. The kind that will make you climax with your clothes on. The passion was off the meter from the both of us. The deeper he went, the deeper I wanted him to go. It was never enough. No one had ever made me feel the way he did. It was the kind of sex that would make you do stupid things you know are wrong…the kind that will make you stay in a bad relationship when you know you need to leave it alone. The kind that will even make you date a married man against your better judgment. That night was the beginning of many lessons to be learned from my experience with KD. Little did I know what lessons those would turn out to be.

In 1998, the sex went on as often as we could make it happen. We didn't care where or when it went on—at the honeycomb hideout, my apartment, hotels, my friends' apartments and homes, in the car, at my job, wherever, whenever. For a while it was just **too** much. We never dated, we never met for lunch or dinner, it was just sex. I didn't want any attachments; being with him was easy and on my terms. I felt as if I could control it.

KD thought he could have any woman he wanted, and he was right. He was married, living a single life. He had sex with *many* other women. I knew I wasn't the only one, but that didn't bother me because at that point it was purely sexual.

As time progressed I figured dating a married man would be easier—on my terms, no commitment, and he couldn't hurt me because I already knew what I was getting into. He couldn't tell me what to do, where to go, or who to see. I didn't have to love him or need him, and he would only be there when we needed each other, it was a safe bet. So while I never sought out to date a married man, it wasn't a deterrent either…it was always a game to see how far I could get. I knew he would have other priorities aside from me, like his wife, career, and at some point children. And for those reasons, I was OK with that. It was just easier. It was a cop-out from dealing with the real issues within me, but having companionship on some dysfunctional level as well.

Then, in 1999, getting past the great sex began to happen, and we started to really get to know each other. We became friends. Almost like best friends, we were open with each other, honest, and vulnerable. What we liked/disliked, some surface issues with his marriage—why he cheated, did he want children and why he didn't have any yet—his career path, his friends, the tragic death of his mother in the mid '90s, and everything else. He was a womanizer and I knew it, but I accepted him for the same reasons he was having sex with me, companionship with no attachment. Why would a married man need companionship? That's a damned good question isn't it?

That was the year KD told me he loved me. I knew he meant it, and not because he said it first, but because he did—and I was everything to him that his wife wasn't. I couldn't believe it. I'd been feeling it for months but I wouldn't give him the satisfaction of a checkmate. It was very emotional, and I told him I loved him, too. We made love that night for the first time and the tears just flowed. I don't know where they came from, but it felt so good and scary at the same time. I didn't have any expectations because I didn't want to "feel" anything. We were moving into an element that couldn't be controlled by either of us.

I wanted him to know I loved him without judgment; that he could be honest with me at all costs. I always accepted KD for who he was; the man, the womanizer, the lover, the friend. I gave him every emotional part of me that he needed. Whatever the wife wouldn't or couldn't give him, I'd been more than happy to. Not because I wanted him to leave her; that didn't come into play. I just loved him and wanted him to be happy, with or without me. I gave him the type of love I wanted for myself. He gave it back; it was multidimensional.

And the fact was, he'd always cheated. He was addicted to women and sex, period. He could not say no. Women were his weakness. He and his wife had only been married six months when we met, and the truth was he was never faithful to her before they married or during the marriage. He said he married her because he loved her and she gave him an ultimatum. He didn't want to lose her, so he did what many men do—get married before they are truly ready. I never doubted his love for her because I could feel it. I knew he wished at times that she would treat him the way did. I could feel myself being used to fill a need, a void. Even though intellectually I knew I was pawn, being with him felt so damn good, so I continued.

Journal entry—September 18, 2000

"I saw KD just a few days ago. We had a very intimate, passionate, and loving night. I love him so much. I know he loves me, too. He is having problems in his marriage and I wish I knew what they were. We have no need to discuss them, just be there for one another. We were talking yesterday and he asked me to go to church with him! I know he means well, but I can't sit in the house with my married lover."

It sounds so silly and stupid reading that now—eleven years later. Just young and dumb but in love no less. Now, you'd have to be wondering where the wife is in all of this; after all, they had no children (yet) and both were transplants from other states. In the beginning, I couldn't understand why in the hell she continued to be with this man. He would stay out **all** night and was so disrespectful and selfish in his actions towards her. I was always amazed at the lengths he'd go through to make his stories believable. The things he and I did together were so wrong—she'd call him on his cell, she'd ask him where he was, and he'd make up a lie, claiming to be with a friend in need of a ride home or that he'd gotten too drunk to drive home and had to stay over at XYZ friend's house. The games he played with her were unbelievable to me, but I didn't care about her so I didn't care that he lied to her. I thought she was a fool because I would **never** put up with him and his disappearing acts. I don't know if she *really* believed him or not, but I'm sure she wanted to. What woman wouldn't? He was always sweet and talked to her so convincingly. He always told her he loved her before he hung up the phone, giving the illusion that he couldn't possibly be with anyone else. Quite the contrary.

The fact was I knew he loved her, and for whatever reason, his life with her didn't matter to me one bit. The fact that she was at home possibly waiting for him didn't trigger regret. How selfish of me. How could I just not given a damn? I was so disconnected from my respect for men, and there was no room for other women's consideration.

Sure, I dated other men, fell in love with other men, slept with other men, and was in relationships with other men during this span, but I always, always loved KD, always. The love was so thick; we could feel it through the phone, through a voice mail, even in silence. Talk about being in love with the wrong man. We literally were in an emotionally attached relationship with each other. It was toxic. It was addictive—I've never done any hard core drugs but I would imagine it was comparable to crack. There were periods where we couldn't get enough of each other.

Journal entry—December 17, 2000
"I don't know what kinda day this has turned out to be. First off, I paged KD and he calls me back from his house. We talked for three hours. I told him I was planning to leave Dallas on January 18, 2001, and he wasn't surprised at all. He was very concerned for my emotional well-being (living with Bianca) and Shania. KD is a good person. We talked about everything under the sun like it was our first time (talking). From me not getting married to sex, men, women, love, God, peace, happiness—about a lot of things. The first time we made love on July 27, which is the day after he lost his mom in '96. He has a business trip planned in Virginia in January and we want to spend it together. It's so hard to let him go. I want to feel this way about my own man (someday). I can't believe I will wake up and see his face (in Virginia). I hope it becomes a reality. He wants to see me so bad and so do I—I just want to hold him."

I know, I can hardly stand it myself. Crazy ramblings of a twenty-three-year-old girl. I can smell the desperation now, but it's hard to see when you're in the middle of it—especially when it's being fed by something you want. He was feeding it, well. It's easier to let something go when it hurts you, but when it feels soo good; it's the hardest, no matter how wrong it is.

The year 2001 was a blur...I don't know where KD was or what was going on with him. I was beginning to leave him in the past—moving on with my life and putting him behind me. It was time to move forward with my life—I was in a good place.

In 2002 somehow we reconnected. OK, I can't take it!! KD and I have been back in communication for months now, talking mostly every day. I'm going to Dallas to see him soon. His wife, Toy, is going to be in Portland, Sacramento, somewhere visiting her sister. He says she might be moving there; perfect.

Several airport terminals, phone calls, and reservations later, I made it to Dallas! As I was standing outside baggage claim waiting for him to pull up, there was a knot in my throat so thick I could choke on it. Not because I was feeling any guilt, but because I loved him dearly. I was so nervous and feeling unusually emotional. It had been about two years since we'd seen each other. I stood there in anticipation with nervous energy. It's funny, no matter how many hours, days, weeks, or years went by without speaking, we always, always, always picked up right where we left off.

"Whew, there he is," I said softly under my breath.

I could see him smiling through the windshield as he pulled up to the curb. My eyes began to well up with tears. He got out and put my bags in his car as I hopped in, then we embraced. Let me explain that moment—I had never felt the way I did that day in my life. The emotion was so incredibly overwhelming; I could not speak or control it. Tears just flowed endlessly…the connection was so strong between the both of us; I cried in his lap all the way to our destination. That has never happened to me in my life, ever. There were no words, only:

"I'm happy to see *you*, too, baby," he said. "I love you, girl, forever."

Now, what I am about to say next is going to piss off every wife, fiancée, and girlfriend reading these pages; and possible some men too. Rightfully so: we were breaking rules, being careless and selfish. We wanted what we wanted, and nothing else or no one else mattered when we were in *those moments*. Why is he married? I thought. God, I wish he wasn't married. This feeling is so perfect.

We pulled up to *their* home, into the garage, and through the back door with my bags we went. That was the first time I'd been in their home. Before we could make it past the office/guest room, we embraced; he kissed me for what seemed like a minute for each day we'd been apart. He grabbed me and held me tight, and then he said something that I never forgot as he held my face with his hands and looked in my eyes.

"You belong here."

I was emotionally done, spent. I mean, seriously, at that point I had been dealing with this man off and on, more on than off, for about five years...and to hear him say that, I just remember feeling weak. I really wanted to throw up. It was no longer a game—I just wanted him. This is when I began to think about his wife and what she might be going through or feeling. I knew that if I, his mistress, could be feeling this deeply, I could only imagine what Toy could be feeling. I was in her house—such a violation, in this woman's house, by her husbands invitation. But it didn't matter...I loved him and didn't care.

"I know," I whispered.

We made love in the middle of the family room floor in that moment— tears from us both and emotions were exhaustive. We were out of our minds—but it felt so good. Where in the hell were my morals and self-respect? Where was his? What was he thinking bringing me to their home, and why on earth would I let him? I'll tell you where our morals and self-respect were; on a plane with the wife on the west coast—no where to be found and too far away to be heard.

Between 2003 and 2005, I'd moved to St. Louis and was in a "committed" relationship with Nick, which we'll talk about in the next Chapter. We subsequently found out Nick and KD were close college buddies. It's a small world for sure.

All of the years up until this point were thick, but the next few years were the thickest between KD and me, and we were not even living in the same city. We talked every day. I mean without fail. Every day on our way to work in the mornings and several times throughout the day. Emotionally I was cheating on Nick with KD. I wasn't happy with Nick, and KD was always there. I was absent, disconnected. I only had enough to give to one man, and at times that was too much to give.

Eventually we were just great friends—we knew that we could count on each other to be honest and be there for one another no matter who we were with. That never failed. KD told me things that broke my heart, and I still loved him through it.

Then KD's wife got pregnant. I was a little surprised because they saw a fertility doctor to make that happen, so it was intentional and how dare I have the right to be angry? Their relationship was so toxic at that time I couldn't understand **why** they would do it. But who was I—nobody! How could I be upset about that, regardless if their relationship was toxic? She *was* still his wife, and he was still her husband. I had to get over it real quick. Toy was hospitalized for months until the delivery. I was happy for him and her that they were bringing life into the world. They had two beautiful children together, and I wanted it to be me. I was a fool and I would have done it, with no questions asked. At that point, for me, it was more about his happiness than my perceived happiness with him. Even though I never understood why they were together, I did know that we would never be—and I was OK with that.

I saw how he easily lied to Toy all the time, and I always would say, "Be honest with her. Tell her the truth, tell her what you really want, and tell her what you really need." I don't know if he did or didn't, but I wanted him to. He had a major void to be filled and would never be faithful until he dealt with that. I knew he wanted to, he just couldn't. And even though we loved each other, I **truly** wanted them to work. I went so far as to buy her Valentine's gifts (baby clothes, candles, etc.) while she was in the hospital during her pregnancy—down to picking the card and the gift wrapping. Like a fool I also purchased the car seats from their registry after discussing it with him. I mean, I loved him, he was my friend, and he was happy about becoming a new father. It wasn't a major decision; I just did what I'd do for anyone expecting a baby. Well, maybe not. I went over board.

After the twins were born Toy contacted me via phone and e-mail. She sent me a thank-you card for the gifts I'd bought the twins while she was in the hospital. And I didn't give her the satisfaction of speaking with her or responding. I had no desire to directly hurt her even though I realized I was hurting her indirectly by carrying on this *relationship* with her husband. She thought he and I knew each other prior to them getting married and that it was some long-distance thing, but that wasn't the case. She really had it all wrong.

I'd flown out to see him during these times, spent New Year's Eve with him, and flown in on other occasions. During their financial strain time, I sent him hundreds of dollars in gift cards over and over for gas, groceries, or whatever—things for the babies—like I said, out of control! I did those things out of friendship and mainly because, I loved him.

I had spoken to KD early one particular morning, and literally a couple of hours later, I got this e-mail from Toy.

toy <█@yahoo.com> wrote: Tue, July 5, 2005 11:20:54 AM
Re: Act like a Lady not a desperate Slut!!!!!!

Aprille,

Listen up, girlfriend. I've been nothing but patient with you and KD's sneaky yet freaky little shit. Not only did he allow you to disrespect our family by sending car seats to our home and lying about the shit. You and KD have continued this little long-distance relationship via e-mail and phone. I must admit, at first I honestly just thought you were some lost and confused freaky slut (judging by the e-mails you've been sending my husband over the years!!). Yes! I've seen those and have copies to show my attorneys! But now I see that you've been keeping in contact and trying to keep track of how his marriage is going. Well, now you know, Ho! I just wish you could have been woman or should I say man enough to talk with me one on one about the matter. But that's what people like you and KD do. Not only have you and other women helped end his marriage of seven and a half years!!!!! You've also altered the lives of his children, which he's only going to be able to see on a long-distance basis.

But, you know what, Aprille What goes around most definitely comes around, so when something happens to you tenfold!!!!! Please remember the Smith family. I really wish I could've spoken to you, possibly over the phone. Unfortunately, your cowardly ass wouldn't even answer your phone that time I tried calling you back from KD's cell. Yeah, remember the time you called KD's cell and I answered? You weren't even woman enough to answer your phone when I tried calling your nasty ass back. And just to think, I honestly thought KD had told your ass then to stop calling... The both of you sorry and confused motherfuckers can have one another.... after all this shit is over and done. I really hope it was worth KD's family departing, since you say you love and need him so much, right?

I deserved this *more* than she could **ever** know. Had she known the depth of what we were really doing, compounded with the other women, she would have been further crushed. Then again maybe she already knew and just wanted confirmation, I don't know. I wasn't mad or angry at this e-mail because I knew I was wrong. I knew she was desperate for answers, and a part of me wanted to give them to her, but I just couldn't. And even though he wasn't loyal to her or me, I was to him. In my mind, had I confessed to her, it would have been with malicious intentions, and it was never about her for me—so I had no reason to "confess" anything. I promised KD I'd never tell her, and I kept that promise. He trusted me to be honest with him—and honestly, there was nothing she could have said to me that would have made me tell her a word. He needed to be the one to be honest with her, not me. Her vows were with him. I didn't feel like I owed her anything at the time.

Truthfully, this <u>entire</u> book could have been about this one relationship but I'll end it with this:

From: Aprille <aprille███@yahoo.com>
To: K█████ <k███08@yahoo.com>Wed, December 6, 2006 12:43:49 PM
Re: Truth

In past years I have not always respected your decision to remain with Toy but I accepted it. I tried not to want too much from you to protect my own feelings. Therefore, I tried to move on in hopes that the love I have for you would go away so that I could move on with my life and give someone all the love I have to give. I would have hoped that if the opportunity even presented itself, then we would be. But what I am conflicted on is, is that realistic? I know that in my heart, I could never be the "other woman" to you again. Because what that would mean is that I was only "just good enough" and nothing more.

∾✶∾

And that's exactly what happened about a year or so after that e-mail: when the opportunity was there, he didn't take it. Mistresses are always "just good enough" for a lot of things, just not the most important things. I like to use the analogy that if he died, no one would have known to call me, because that's how much I mattered in "real life." While the love was beautiful and I learned so much from the experience, the truth was, I was a placeholder—filling in a void and nothing more. In real life, I didn't matter. There would be no family gatherings, birthday parties, or important holidays....I played myself.

In the end, they divorced, and he and I remained "friends." It's my understanding that they have a good relationship today.

There are no words to explain how apologetic I am for causing strife in their marriage and the level of disrespect I had towards her. While I know there were <u>many</u> other women, I know my relationship with KD played a role—whether she knew to what level or not is a mystery to me and is irrelevant. To this day, Toy and I have never spoken; I reached out prior to writing this book to speak with her, but too little, too late. I often ask myself, do I think <u>I</u> ruined their marriage? I know for sure it would have ended without my involvement with him, but I also acknowledge that I played a role in his distraction from her for almost their entire marriage. So, my answer is: yes, in part.

I wish KD the very best that life has to offer.

∾✶∾

There were many lessons to be learned through this twisted web of betrayal and deception. Aside from the elephant in the room, which is "don't date married men," it's a dead end to nowhere. What I learned was never to lose myself in a person again. **That** was the issue. My judgment was so off because I lost myself before I even knew who I truly was. I put

KD's happiness in front of mine more than he'll ever know. Instead of dealing with me, I dealt with him, and that turned into, as Toy implied, a desperate kind of love. Had I been whole and elevated my standards, he would have never gotten past the initial "I'm married and my wife is the most important thing to me" phone call.

CHAPTER
8

THE MAN WISH LIST
BE CAREFUL WHAT YOU WISH FOR

"Your intuition never lies.
You lie to your intuition."

—THE LUVOLOGIST

Generally speaking, our standards and expectations we set for men are all different based on two things. One is our view of what a good man is or should be. These ideas were developed from what you witnessed, missed out on, or from your past relationship experiences with men. It seems to me that standards are developed from what we think or what we imagine, and not so much from what we know for sure. I say that because we know several things for sure, and then go against them anyway. The truth is, none of us know really what we're doing. We pray, hope, and wish we make the right choices based on what we've learned NOT to do through our past mistakes and from situations that have made us uncomfortable in the past. But we often repeat the same cycles even when we know better.

The second, more important issue with standards that women hold men to revolves around our self-esteem, self-love, and of self-worth; or lack thereof. Many times the standards you set for men are a direct reflection of what you currently think about yourself, regardless of your economic status, education, or other areas in your life that you're most proud of. In most cases, you are dating your self-esteem. This is why you find women repeating the same mistakes over and over again, wondering why we keep ending up with the same type of men, and asking ourselves why we keep attracting the same type of men again and again. It's because you are still the same woman. Most times the standards a woman say she wants in a man, her expectations, and what she's willing to put up with, don't match. Setting the standards mentally or putting them on paper means nothing if you're really not expecting men to meet them in the first place.

I'd be willing to bet that many of the women you see walking around don't feel that great about themselves. They/we may never admit it, but I think it's true. They are missing the number one key component to any relationship, and that's the relationship they have with the woman in the mirror. We are just going through the motions, putting on a happy "date me" face. We know it's a requirement to have standards, but we still continue to date men outside of those standards because we don't *truly* believe we deserve the best. Women expect what they think they deserve. And when you don't think you deserve much, you end up flocking to or remaining in bad relationships. Seemingly having it all materially doesn't mean you have it all together. There are plenty of successful women with dysfunctional relationships and poor dating skills.

Most women want to be with a man that can fulfill the traditional role of what a man should be in a relationship, regardless of where she is in her life—how successful she is or independent she claims to be. But that doesn't mean she's living by the standard she sets, wants, or desires. Sure, you can make a meaningless list of characteristics and wants, and I understand the importance of making lists, having affirmative thoughts, the law of attraction, faith, positive thinking, etc. But none of those things make a difference if we're all jacked up on the inside.

I must confess...

"I'll create a higher standard for the men I come in contact with in the future. I'll take some time to focus on me. I won't hold any bitterness in my heart from my past and will accept responsibility for my part." Moving on I thought as I said my desperation prayer, again asking God to forgive and save me from myself, promising to make better choices tomorrow.

The list of "what I want in a man" that my old preacher told all the women in church to write down when I was nineteen has resonated with me throughout the years. My sentiment and I had placed my list in my journal for safekeeping. As the years went on, I lost the list several times, and when that happened, I just scribbled down a new one. Finally, in my mid twenties, I made "the final list," and it followed me until just a few years ago. My original "man wish list" had thirty or so words on it. I say "words" because that all they were—they didn't mean a damn thing. I wasn't ready for half of the characteristics I'd written down—hell; I didn't even think such a man existed in real life. Over the years I'd go back to the list and actually cross off things that I didn't "have to have," as some traits became less important to me. And I'd add things that I found out I wanted during my trial-and-error dating sagas as well.

> As we mature and evolve as women, our needs will change and so do our expectations of others. If you're not evolving, you're not growing and that may just be the problem.

Here was some of my original list: "Funny, smart, wants children or more children, attractive, six foot or taller, health conscious, financially stable, has a career, has to be a great lover, gets along with his parents, has goals, is affectionate, never been to prison, accepts my daughter as his own, compassionate, giving, unselfish, has his own home, has a sense of humor, can make me laugh, is a good tipper (to service workers), has no more than one child, has never been married," and the list went on and on. Whew!

I never really met my wish-list man through those years, but I'd meet bits and pieces of him. Sometimes it took two or three men to complete the whole list. Then there were times when I was just wasting time so I wouldn't have to be alone, knowing they didn't measure up at all. Nevertheless, I wasn't satisfied with them. Sure, I had loved some wonderful men and had some great times; and experiences I wouldn't change for anything in the world. But deep down, I kept *hoping* I'd meet the man from my list without realizing my part in why I wasn't meeting him. Or maybe I *had* met him, and ran him off or didn't recognize him. What ever the case it was like I was expecting to find him with each new guy I'd meet, hoping that *he* was it. I often doubted my standards and sometimes felt maybe I was being too demanding or unrealistic. Maybe I shouldn't be so picky I'd think to myself. Maybe he just needs to have the basics. But it was drilled into my head that I'd be settling if I didn't get all of the things I wanted. Then I'd actually have friends say, "A piece a man is better than no man at all." Oh, noooo, I couldn't subscribe to that back then, and I sure as heck don't today.

> There is no such thing as a *piece of a man*. If you think there is you're dealing with a piece of you. Work on becoming more whole, more of your authentic self, every day.

After going through the hurts, disappointments, and bad decisions of yesteryear, when I was in my mid-twenties I made a vow to myself that I *would* give love a chance if it ever presented itself again. I wouldn't let my past experiences affect my future happiness. I would no longer let it define who I was. I figured I could love anybody, right? Aren't we designed that way? I mean, we're emotional beings. Besides, that's what they used to do back in the old days. The marriage of a young woman would be arranged with a man once she hit puberty. The love would come later; the work and family would come first. They had to learn compatibility, and they'd remain married until death did them part. I just needed to *like* a man who met my standards; most of the things on my list. Right? I wish it were that simple.

Fast forward a couple of years just six days before September 11, 2001. I was sitting in the parking lot of the Mobile Regional Airport waiting for my boss, who was renting a car for a sporting event that was in town. The Black American Softball Association, to be exact. As I was waiting (minding my own business), a guy approached my vehicle; we'll call him Nick. At first glance he wasn't the type of guy I'd normally entertain but admittedly there was something charismatic about him. I was my usual nonchalant self. He humored me and told me he was visiting from St. Louis with the tournament. So that was our common thread for the moment, and, after some small talk, he asked if we could have dinner while he was in town. Before I could decide about dinner, he said that he'd love to fly me to St. Louis for a visit. I may have been young but I wasn't easily impressed by what a man could do for me; I'd already seen what they could do. I learned to work hard and always took the attitude that what a man has is his until you're married. I was more concerned with whether he kept his word and did things when he said he'd do them for me, no matter how big or small it was. It was more about honor for me. I'd already lived too many lies by this stage of the relationship game to get caught up with diamonds and pearls (so to speak). I wanted something real if I was going to put any effort into it.

His arrogance was a bit intriguing, so I agreed to dinner; we exchanged numbers and talked a bit more. *I don't know what's up with me and arrogant men.* He soon went on his way. Later that day he called; I remember sitting on my mother's sofa watching his name flash across the phone as it rang. I didn't answer it because I wasn't sure I wanted to be bothered. I knew he'd be headed back to St. Louis in just a day or two, so what would be the point? I wasn't interested in having a long-distance relationship (LDR) either. My life was there in Mobile and I was doing all right for myself. It's where I began my asset management career. Long story short, our plans to meet while he was in in town never came about.

A few days after 9/11, Nick called to ask when he could fly me to St. Louis since he missed his opportunity to meet with me while he was in town. The Federal Aviation Administration (FAA) had put a screeching halt to air travel, and at that time no one knew when it would resume again. No one wanted to fly and I was in no hurry. Eventually, I agreed to come and see him once air travel was cleared for safety. I have to mention, he worked for the airlines, so my ticket could have been free. The snob in me at the time refused to travel on his airline because I had miles racked up with another carrier. Thinking back, that was just my way of controlling the situation, because I refused to let a man have his way. I wanted a man to take the lead, but I got in the way of it all the time; I was too afraid of what *might* happen. The more of the situation I could control, the less of me he could control. I'd do what he wanted eventually, but not without having it my way first. I was too independent for that and the unknowns were too scary.

September 28, 2001, we were cleared for travel, if you want to call it that—and that was the most scared I'd been on any plane in my entire life. Nonetheless, I went. As I boarded the plane, I thought, let's see where this goes! This would be my first visit to St. Louis. It's just a visit, we would keep it light. I didn't know how he'd measure up with my standards totally because we'd only talked on the phone. I did enjoy being pursued, and his persistence was a plus. Like I said earlier, I wanted a man to do what he said he would do. "Passengers, the captain has turned on the 'fasten seat belt' sign." And off I went.

After a couple of hours and one stopover in Memphis, I arrived in St. Louis safe and sound. Nick was waiting for me inside the terminal at the baggage claim. He greeted me with a hug, grabbed my bags, and off we went. He had the weekend filled with touristy things to do, which was great, because there's nothing worse than being asked out by a man and then he can't think of anything to do! "Be creative, have a plan" was my motto. This was my first visit to St. Louis so I was excited about it and I genuinely love to travel to new places. As the weekend progressed, we had some great talks about relationships and where we were in our own lives at the time. He was three months fresh out of a three-year relationship, which he clearly wasn't over because he still had pictures of his ex girlfriend up everywhere in his apartment. I wrote that off because who was I to question him? I thought we were both pretty transparent, which was my style— it gave me the right to ask anything I felt I needed to know. At that time I had just begun my career and was headed on a great path professionally— and if I was willing to lay my cards on the table and be truthful, then any potential mate would have to do the same. I even went so far as to ask him how much money he made. He didn't blink, and wrote it down on a little piece of paper. I remember telling him, "I can work with that." I was real sassy. As I think back, I don't know how anyone put up with me at times.

Never get in a relationship with a man who just broke up with anyone, or who is recently separated or newly divorced! You <u>are</u> wasting your time. He is thinking about her every time he says your name. Men need time to get over us just like we need time to get over them. Don't be a place holder for any man.

After that visit and several subsequent visits to St. Louis, I discovered Nick was in fact most of the things on my list. He was what I called "paper perfect." You know, when something or someone looks great on paper. Good credit, good job, gets along with his mother, had only one son, loved to travel, was well received, liked amongst his peers, and so on—most of what a woman would want based on those facts alone. I figured as long as I *liked* him, we could work on the rest. Nick was the type of man a woman was supposed to marry—on paper. And because I was little jaded from my past experiences, I removed the "how I feel" part of the picture (because feelings hadn't worked for me in the past) and became more focused on meeting a man that met the list of standards. I wanted to make sure we could work logistically. I figured the feelings would develop more over time as we got to know each other—I was okay with that. After all, I did kinda like him at that point.

After several months of three-hour phone calls and frequent-flyer miles between Mobile and St. Louis, we decided to begin our long-distance relationship. Let me just say the dynamics for that to be a success in itself took a higher level of commitment and communication than I knew or was ready for. Also, my plans to relocate back to Dallas were deferred in a major way—Nick wasn't leaving his comfort zone—OK, his mama—in St. Louis. So it became my home away from home. Eventually I knew I'd have to move there, and I was OK with that as long as the relationship was progressing in a positive way.

During the long distance part of our relationship, many things came to the surface between us. Nick was controlling, just the opposite of what I wanted. He called me at least six to eight times a day—even thought I didn't particularly like it I was young and chalked it up to mean meant he must really love me. After a while I began to expect it and allowed myself to think it was normal behavior. There was something else about him, but I couldn't put my finger on it at the time. At that point I was developing true feelings for him and didn't want to risk losing him, so I dismissed it. That was the first real relationship I'd been in…I mean, there was Ryan and KD, but we all know what happened there. Being with Nick forced me to grow up in ways I didn't know I needed to.

After the first year we began making plans for me to seriously relocate to St. Louis. And within the next year it had come to fruition. To tell the truth, I felt in the pit of my stomach that moving there would be a mistake. I absolutely didn't like some of his ways, but some parts of him were really good. I loved the *idea* of what we could have been together, not necessarily *us* together. I kept in mind the 80/20 rule then remembered that vow I made to myself just the year before to "give love a chance," so my relocation journey to St. Louis began. I started my job search, he began looking for a place that would accommodate Shania and me, we set up bank accounts, and then just like that, it was happening. Within a few months, he and a couple of buddies had driven down to Mobile and rented a moving trailer to transport all of my things in advance. He had **all** of my stuff in *our* new place. There was definitely no turning back! I always did what I committed to; failure was not an option.

After almost two years to the month, the move became a reality. I remember stalling at my parents' house and not wanting to leave like it was just yesterday. I didn't leave until after 5 p.m. …just hanging around as if I didn't have a eleven-hour drive ahead of me. I finally got on the road with Shania and was St. Louis bound. I arrived in the wee hours of the morning. By the time I got there, I figured it might be a good idea. I was always attracted to new places and experiences. That next morning I hit the ground running and within two weeks I'd found a position in my field, and that made me feel good about the transition. Making a contribution and doing my part was always important to me. Nick was happy about that, too, as if I had validated the promises I made to him before I arrived. After all, this was it—we were *really* a couple, in the same state-city-house.

It was different being with Nick on a daily basis; up until that point, the most time we'd spent together in two years was maybe a week. It didn't take long for me to realize my gut feeling was real and I didn't want to be with him. He was an asshole, and not in that sexy dry-humor kind of way either. But I was there now, and I'd left my job and life back in Mobile to "give love a chance." So that's what I did.

One good thing about Nick and I, we were a good business team. We **gelled** in that regard. We were both successful in our own right and lived a comfortable lifestyle. We even started a real estate business together. We had everything we wanted, traveled anywhere we desired. Even during a period of him being laid off after working for the airline for almost ten years, I encouraged him to take off six months because he *deserved* it. Financially we had no issues, so *that* stress wasn't present, but there was something deeper that was constantly looming over us.

Control, manipulation, mind games and we argued a couple of times per week. He knew he was all I had there and used that every chance he got. The only freakin' reason I moved to St. Louis was to be with him—had I followed *my* plan, I'd have been back in Dallas already! Like in any relationship, you share private things with your mate, so I'd confess things that had occurred in my past (like I'm doing now), and he'd throw them in my face later if we were arguing. Every chance he got. He didn't fight fair at all. I got thrown under the bus by my own man on many occasions. I'd express how badly that hurt me and that he was killing me slowly—he'd apologize, promise not to do it again, then we'd kiss and make up. But that only lasted until he did it again.

To make matters worse, on the outside he dogged me out to his friends and tried to make it seem like I was the crazy one, when in actuality it was him. He was emotionally abusive to me, tearing me down every chance he got. He had to be the one to look good to everyone on the outside. I never met a grown man more consumed with being **popular** in my life. We argued almost every single day, about something. As time went on he became physically abusive—careful not to hit me in my face. But he'd punch me into the fetal position in any given corner. He was the type of man that would destroy my personal property—anything. Throwing things like my laptop, cell phone, and anything else that belonged to me that he could get his hand on. His actions made me violent, too. I was on the defensive all the time, so I'd throw things at him. He could make me furious. And keep in mind; I was so adamant about never being trapped like other abused women. Being put in a position to **have** to take that type of abuse was crazy talk. Just so I am clear, he was a mind gamer, the physical was not often but it did happen. Nick was about mind control and breaking me down.

On top of that I didn't have any of my own friends there, only his circle, so I felt very alone. I couldn't tell anyone, because, well, I was too "happy and together" on the outside to admit I was in that type of situation. I already had little respect for men at this point, and he just added fuel to the fire. He disrespected everything I asked of him as my man. One thing I stressed over and over was that I refused to argue in front of my daughter; because of my upbringing, I **never** wanted her to see that. But he'd intentionally do it anyway; he knew it hurt me to the core. He used my daughter as a pawn, and I hated him for that.

As time went on, I didn't know what I was going to do. This relationship hurt me because I'd given up so much to be with him, and *this* is what he was. Don't get me wrong, we had some happy moments sprinkled in here and there. There was some love and plans for a future. So every day wasn't a bad day. But when they were bad, damn, they were bad. My spirit was broken into little bitty pieces. I couldn't believe my paper-perfect relationship was like a bad dream. When I realized that Nick could make promises and the next week I'd be a "stupid muthafucker," I didn't care anymore. And not only that, but when I realized I was

> Have you ever been miserable in a relationship but the other person you were in it with was happy, and he or she couldn't see what the problem was? You are not equally yoked, on the same page, or headed in the same direction. Get out now!

never willing to give him 100 percent of me because I didn't trust him with my heart; I knew it was time to make a change. Emotionally, we were on empty—running on fumes. And for me, that was the most important component of any relationship—I had to have it and still do. Once I knew he could misuse that without regards for my feelings or well-being, what I did no longer mattered.

And like many people in bad relationships, I became a habitual cheater *within* the relationship, looking on the outside for what I was missing. This is the first time I have admitted it. KD and I rekindled an emotional affair, and I depended on him to fulfill my needs from a distance, which he did. People underestimate the power of an emotional affair—but they are the **most** dangerous. Sex was minuscule in comparison—emotions are what drive people to do things that make absolutely no sense at all.

There were several occasions that KD and I were together during this time span. I'd fly to Dallas, drive to Dallas, whatever it took to get my needs fulfilled. On one occasion I'd flown to Dallas and Nick didn't even know I was there—I'd be home just in time to cook dinner as if I'd been at work all day. Scandalous, sure it was. But I was starving for something—and when you're starving, you'll do just about anything to get fed. Like the blood flowing through my veins, attention and love were food for me. I don't know if Nick was unfaithful to me, and I didn't care if he was because I was emotionally checked out. In order to deal with him, I had to be. And if he told me today that he was unfaithful our entire relationship, I wouldn't blink, not even once. I hate to admit this, but I've never been as unhappy with a man as I was when I was with Nick. Through everything, he was emotionally too much for this woman to deal with. His intentions weren't in my favor.

I reverted back to my younger, promiscuous years. I was looking for love in all the wrong places. I had several flings with different people and an affair with a co-worker during the course of our relationship. In my mind, I was single—just waiting for an opportunity to leave Nick. But I didn't leave him, and for some reason I thought I still wanted to be with him, as if we could change *together.* And through all of that I still agreed to do everything to save that relationship. Silly me. We weren't even married, but I was committed to making it work; we even went to couples counseling, where I would later discover that he didn't feel love growing up or hear it, which is why he didn't know how to show it to me. We didn't finish couples counseling because I think it was too real for him. I kept going and began my own road to recovery to deal with my past. So while he blamed me for the failure of our relationship, he had issues he needed to deal with as well. Like a broken record, he'd say over and over that I wasn't ready to be in a relationship, and that would get under my skin because I knew neither was he! BUT I can now admit he was right about one thing: I wasn't ready for what he had to give. It would have never worked because I was never in it totally, I was too afraid to trust him and he demanded respect he didn't earn.

The sad and weakest part about the whole relationship was he never took ownership of his part in it; everything was my fault until the very end. If you asked him today, it would still be my fault; he did **nothing** wrong. He's perfect. The only word I can use to describe how frustrating it is to be with a man who refuses to take responsibility for his actions is not even a real word—so I won't use it.

At that time I'd come up with "Operation A"—which was code between my friends and me for "I'm leaving his ass as soon as I can!" And after nearly five years of Nick, me moving out and attempting to leave, then letting him back into my life and moving into the bedroom with my daughter, it was over one evening in the middle of the night. I couldn't take it anymore. I couldn't stand to look at him, and I am sure he was tired of looking at me. We were both tired of going round and round about the same things…year after year. I wanted out.

Leaving was the easy part…not falling into my own weaknesses about being alone was hard to deal with. My mind played tricks on me months after the breakup, making me think I wanted him back. I even remember begging him to get back together at one point. And for what?? It was one of those pathetic moments I'd be too embarrassed to tell my friends or family I had. There I was, reducing my standards for the sake of being with a man who treated me like crap. Thankfully we never reentered into a relationship with each other again even though we tried to be friends. But I knew it really would never work because he hadn't changed.

I take full responsibility for getting involved with Nick under false pretenses. I wanted the fairy tale when I wanted it, regardless of whether I was ready for it or not. And even though we communicated a lot in the beginning, it wasn't the right type of communication about the right things. I dismissed every red flag that tugged on my intuition telling me something wasn't right, just for the chance that someone (Nick) would love me in the way I needed him to. I needed to work on me, find my own worth, and begin to love myself without a man involved. Nick and I would have never worked, but I needed the experience to help me grow into the woman I am today. So, for that I am grateful.

I learned that most of the time we have good intentions and that *situations* don't seem much like **situations** at the time you decide to do something. And other times, we're just fumbling through *hoping* to make the right decisions because we want the *xyz* outcome. Our motives don't really matter—good or bad, right or wrong, we want what we want. I do believe I had realistic expectations, but with the wrong man, wrong circumstances, and wrong time in <u>my</u> life. I remained in that relationship with Nick longer than I should have because he was "paper perfect" and I didn't want us to fail. Correction—I didn't want *me* to fail. I also realized a lot about myself and that I still had a lot growing up to do. I was also hoping he'd evolve into what I truly wanted. Not that I would change him, but that by being with me, somehow he'd want to change. But that never happened while we were together.

⋞✕⋟

In retrospect, my list was important but didn't really matter. Isn't that a misnomer?! It should have reminded me what I really wanted so I wouldn't make the mistake of being with Mr. Wrong or Mr. Right Now longer than I should have. Wrong and Right Now are teaching relationships. I already knew what I wanted, and so did the man upstairs. I was already putting it out there; I just needed to believe I'd receive it, that it would come to me. Stressing and obsessing over my list or singlehood didn't make things happen any faster than they were supposed to. Not that I was stressing, but I did put emphasis on what I **had** to have. I wanted to be happier with a man in my life than without one. I wanted someone to add to what was already there. Someone who could make me an even better woman and person. I knew that when *he* came along and made me feel even better about myself, that would be the man for me.

Allow a man to show you who he is based on his actions. You'll soon see if he's what you want. I soon realized that a man can be all the things on my list and none of what I need. And vice versa, for that matter! For example, I needed a man I could communicate with, who was affectionate, who accepted me for who I was, and the woman I am constantly evolving into. That's really what I wanted, needed.

⋞✕⋟

What Advice I'd give my 20-something self

Don't discount the hardships, breakups, and seemingly bad experiences. If we were meant to turn eighteen and meet the man of our dreams the following day, it would happen that way. The truth is, none of know what we're doing. And just because we have standards that men seem to meet in the beginning doesn't mean they actually will meet them when it gets real. We learn by making mistakes and from situations that make us uncomfortable. From that, we learn what we don't like and what we absolutely do. What we can and won't put up with.

The next time you meet a man, ask yourself what it is about him that appeals to you. What is it about him that doesn't? How does he make you feel? How does he deal with other people? Give him a chance to show you who he is based on his qualities alone. Don't hold him accountable for the actions or inactions of other men. Deal with those realities and decide if that will work for you at this point in your life. There may be things about him that you so enjoy that aren't even on your silly list. Mr. Could Be, maybe Mr. Would Be Mr. Right if you gave him a chance. Don't be one of those women who let a good man get away from you. Now he's Mr. Perfect to some other seemingly undeserving woman and you're in a corner wishing it was you because you were afraid to get to know yourself and be who you are.

De-friend fear when you feel her creeping up into your subconscious. You have to treat each person like you've never been with another man before. And lastly, enjoy the ride.

CHAPTER
9

I DON'T NEED A MAN
I JUST WANT ONE

Being single isn't bad. What is bad is giving up
hope on finding that someone special.

—ANONYMOUS

We've given ourselves a complex with the word _need_. And since independent women have pigeonholed themselves into not asking for help, we
have internalized saying you need anything as a sign of weakness or that
you are off your game—as if it means you'll be more dependent, incapable,
or weak. It's that constant self-defeating validation that you can do all
things on your own without a man, and that a man is only an option. But,
on the other hand, if having a long-term relationship or marriage is what
you want in your life, you need a man to complete the equation. Having
one, a real good one, is more than just an option. As much as you'd hate to
say it out loud, it's the truth. You can't have it both ways. But after dealing
with disappointments over the years, it's hard to utter those words. Who
wants to admit they need something today that's hurt them in the past?

Fear is evil and will make you believe things you know aren't true just to make yourself feel better. It gives you permission to lie to yourself. At some point you have to ask yourself, what are you really afraid of? Fear plays tricks on our hearts and minds. It is the root of so many struggles many women have today. We are afraid to let a man **in** because we do not want to be hurt again and again and again.

The "I don't need a man" mantra seems to be the default response for many women to make *themselves* feel OK about being single, so other people won't think any less of them or think that something is wrong with them because they are single. As if there is something wrong with you because you don't have a man—today. It's that silly need to validate or prove you can do all things without help. You're letting a man know that before he thinks that you need him—you really don't. It's your attempt to remain in control of your heart, your feelings, and what comes into your space. And even if you never verbalize this thought to a man and only think it, it has the same effect within you—sending conflicting messages between your heart and brain. It sets off a little trigger in your mind that, once activated, says:

"I don't want to be vulnerable or let him know that I am, so this 'shield' will protect me from anything he might do wrong in the future. I'll be ready for it and any future disappointments won't affect me in the least bit. If I keep up this façade long enough, I'll believe I really don't need him or any other man."

I told myself this lie for years. I knew I didn't mean it when I said it, but for that moment it made me feel good about some situation that didn't go the way I'd hoped it would. This mind-set is toxic, and it changes how you engage and react in relationships. The problem is, once you say this to yourself or to others, you now have live up to it. Our thoughts and words are powerful...because what I really meant was, "I need a good man in my life, one that won't hurt me, break my heart, disappoint, or lie to me again. I need to be loved."

I find it ironic that as women we're taught **not** to need a man, to do things on our own and we go on saying we don't need one, but men, on the other hand, *need* to be needed by us. An oxymoron if I've ever heard one. No wonder we're all so screwed up. We are not working together. Both are afraid of what the other will do to us when men and women ultimately want the same things; to love and be loved.

I must confess...

After breaking up with Nick and moving out of our apartment in St. Louis, it was back to single parent mode for me. I had been there before, so I just dusted off my landing gear and was ready for whatever came my way. A friend of mine at the time owned a real estate management company, so finding a new place was as simple as making a phone call. I called off work and moved on the opposite side of town the very next day. I didn't have time to deal with the breakup; I had to keep it together and move on. Wow, nearly five years of my life, gone in the middle of the night, literally. For weeks I felt displaced because I had moved to St. Louis to be with Nick, and now it was over. After a few weeks of being out on my own, I was struggling with everything. Not so much financially as it was a juggling act overall; life, the breakup, my career, motherhood, and the relocation. It was closing in on me, but I did a pretty good job *pretending* that things were okay. But something in me couldn't get past the feeling that I had failed my own independent self by needing Nick or anyone else. I suddenly didn't feel so free and independent. My mind was so cloudy I didn't know who I was. The truth was, I felt alone, abandoned, drained. I needed to redefine myself, reinvent who I was, **recharge** my life but who had time for that? I had a daughter to raise, bills to pay, and life was moving on with or without me. I was struggling with "not keeping it together." After all, I had a solid plan and it didn't work out. So now what?

> In my opinion, I'm not sure if balance in life exists. Who wants to attempt a balancing act on a daily basis? Something always gets more attention than something else according to where you are in your journey. Sometimes it's you, the kids, men, and the career but never is it all balanced. I think the key is knowing that—**that** is okay.

Just a couple of months before Nick and I split up, I'd met Mark through a close friend of mine. We were friendly but maintained a platonic relationship while I was with Nick. But as soon as the opportunity arose, we began to see each other. I wasn't ready to be in love or get into another relationship, but, like many times before, I jumped in before I was truly ready, not really dealing with myself or giving myself any alone time. Being alone, not lonely, forces you to think about yourself. And if we think too much, then we begin to feel, and when we feel, the pain comes through.

Mark was a handsome, forty-two-year-old, six-foot-two, creamy chocolate complexioned business owner, a snazzy dancer, and great in *sooo* many other ways. He was a sweetie and would do nice things for me **all** the time; I appreciated them but didn't know how to *receive* him. I wanted to accept it, even needed to at times. But I really didn't want him to think I needed him in any way nor did I want to be in a position where I had to need him. Emotionally or otherwise. I felt if he thought that, I'd lose my ground. I wanted to want him and leave my needs at the door. My emotions were on lockdown but I didn't want them to be. It was a constant struggle for me to let it go.

One beautiful sunny afternoon I came home from work for lunch. I walked in and the first thing I noticed was the scent. It was unfamiliar but refreshing at the same time. I was thinking, "What's going on here?" as I walked up the stairs...my house was spic and span...bed made (I don't do that), kitchen was cleaned from breakfast, and flowers were on my dining room table. Mark had come by my place on his lunch break and tidied up! Sounds like a nice thing to do, huh? At first I didn't think it was a nice gesture at first and was totally pissed off. After a few minutes of me tripping with myself, I called him and asked had he been by, and he said yes. "I thought it would be nice. I know you've been working so hard lately." I immediately when into defense mode; I felt a little violated. I snapped his head off as if he had broken in and stolen something. Not because he had straightened up my house, but because I felt he thought I needed him to help me. How screwed up must I be? That was a major revelation for me. "Aprille, you are losing it. Get it together!" At that time I didn't understand why I was consumed with showing men that I was so strong, but I was beginning to.

When was the last time a man came to your house and cleaned it so you wouldn't have to when you got off work? Independent women want everyone to know that we can handle everything, all the time, even when we can't and things are spiraling out of control. Even when the house is about to go into foreclosure, bankruptcy is a looming reality, and we are at odds with the men in our lives, we still maintain autonomy as if it's gotten us somewhere thus far.

After I hung up the phone, Mark came right over. As soon as he walked through the door and up the stairs, I just broke down in tears in his arms. I was conflicted with his gesture and my reaction. What in the hell is wrong with me, I thought to myself. I wasn't used to asking for anything. And though I didn't ask him to help me, I wanted him to help me. And it wasn't about the cleaning. Silly me.

We had a long, intense talk about that day and he just simply said, "This is what real grown men do. This is what I do." Now, he didn't mean the cleaning part. He meant a good man will give you what you *need* when you need it. That day, I needed to come home and put my feet up without worrying about all the other little things we tend to worry about when we get home. I wanted to let down my guard but I was afraid to let him in for fear of getting hurt—again.

I pondered over my reaction to this for several weeks. Why did I feel so violated? Why did I get defensive when his actions were coming from a loving place? Finally, the answer came to me. I was not in control of it. I didn't ask him to and I didn't know the plan. It wasn't that I didn't want or need his gestures. I truly <u>didn't know how</u> to receive what he was doing because I perceived his actions as if he were saying I was weak. I was so used to doing everything on my own; even in my previous relationship with Nick, I felt the need to constantly prove myself. So I took charge of everything, even when I didn't have to. Strong, independent—confused.

On a separate occasion, Mark called and asked me what bills I had for the month that needed to be paid. I could pay my own bills, I thought. Was I doing something that was indicating that I couldn't? But the truth was, I *was* struggling with my new set of expenses and the ones created during my previous relationship. I told him that he was too kind and thanked him for thinking of me. The truth was, any help would have been put to good use. I was channeling money all over the place to make it work. Mark didn't accept that; he told me I needed a breather. A couple days later he came to my house and gave me the money for my bills that month. He was always doing things that I actually needed him to do; again, I didn't know how to receive him but he was showing me daily.

In that moment he said to me, "You seem ungrateful at times." With a raised brow I was blown away. I was most grateful and thankful, BUT I was so shocked I didn't know how to let go of my being used to being independent and doing for myself. I was waiting for the catch every day—wondering when he was going to come out of the bag and do what every man had done in my past.

"Oh, my goodness, just the opposite. No one has come to me in my time of need. Up until this point I've mostly always done it on my own. Even with that asshole I just left. What you see is amazement, not ungratefulness."

After I explained to him that I was viewed as the strong one of my peers, in control of everything, he simply said, "That was then, this is now. Don't hold me accountable for what other men failed to do. Get over that and get used to me, how I do things." Now that sounds good, right? Well, he meant it and lived up to it while we were together, but it was still an adjustment for me to get used to. I realized I was still carrying the past with me, and was holding him hostage for the things other men had done to me. I wasn't bitter at this point, but I didn't know how to trust or how to release control totally. Fear was in my ear every few days with these "what if" scenarios. Knowing how to receive what you say you want is part of the challenge as well. Mentally I had to check myself and learn to relax and just go with the flow. I was paying attention and learning that sometimes the most unlikely people are put in your life for a period of time, a season, to help you get over a hump. It's like they just fall out of the sky just when you need them the most, I call them 'lifelines.'

One night as I was sleeping, I felt rain drops on my head. My house was surrounded with trees, which had beaten up my roof on the side of my bedroom. It was raining on me, drip, drop, drip! I texted Mark that night to tell him out of shock and a little humor, "Honey, it's raining on my head!"

After moving my bed around, finding a bucket to catch the water, I attempted to drift back to sleep. The next morning came quickly, and Mark came over to look at the damage and told me he knew some roofers. I had to get to work, so we just left it at that and went about our day. There was no forecast for rain, so I knew I had a small window of time to get repairs in order.

I was working at an apartment complex in St. Louis, and I got off around six to head home. When I pulled up to my house, there were three men on my roof—tearing off the old layers, laying down new wood, and making repairs. As I was getting out of my car I asked, "Ummm, who hired you?!" The head guy yelled from the roof, "Mark!" Can I exhale now? Wow. What a man he was…he showed me what a man *will* do when he loves you, and I began to trust a little more and worry a little less with every passing day.

I learned so many lessons from Mark. He taught me that men with good intentions treat women well. And those with not-so-good intentions, well, they don't. And that it was OK to receive it (and shut the hell up). He was endearing, the right amount of sensitive, and made love to me like I was the only woman in the world. I was thirty years old and this was the first man who had made me feel like a *real* woman. He truly taught me how a man is supposed to treat a woman, peeling back layers of doubt. Chivalry does exist. I needed that man like no tomorrow, and I didn't know it at first because I was too busy resisting. I needed his touch, his smell, his kisses, his support, and his love. Once I admitted that to myself, I was beginning to set myself free.

After about a year, we stopped seeing each other, and I was OK with that. There is goodness in most men. Even when they've made some bad choices, there is something to be learned from every experience. I chose to find the good and the lesson in my time with Mark. My standards would be forever raised. I now know that I would always deserve to be treated like the queen within me.

By this point I had totally let go of the attitude that all men are no good and began to soften up. I didn't want to be angry and hold the past against anybody. Bitterness was not a part of me anymore. I loved just "being." God knew I needed something, a sign that all was not doomed. That all of the mess I'd gone through with men in my past wasn't ALL men. So he threw me a lifeline. Not perfect, but it showed me the capabilities and value of having a man around in a positive way.

For the longest time I thought I knew what I needed. Sure, I knew the basics traits I wanted in a man, but it takes another human being, with his experiences, personality, and flaws, to bring out things in me that I didn't know existed. You may not realize it, but the right man will give you things you didn't even know you needed. Don't miss out by thinking you know what all those things are.

And then there was Romey...

"I am not looking for a relationship. I am not looking for a relationship—and with that being the case..."

A girlfriend of mine, Shaun, invited me to a biker party on the Eads Bridge that separates St. Louis from East St. Louis. I remember it being hot, real hot. It was an annual thing so I thought it would be cool to check out. I really wasn't into bikers but I did like bikes and wanted to learn how to ride, so I was in. There had to be hundreds of bikers on the bridge, grilling, playing loud music, just having a real good time. As we were about to get in line to order a drink, a guy walks up and asks us what we were drinking. I'd seen him just moments earlier in passing but I was in an "I don't want to meet anyone" mode, so I kept walking. He came back with our drinks (vodka, cranberry, and a splash of orange juice) and off he went. Now **that** I love—just buy me a drink and don't think my time is worth the $5 you paid for it. As we made our way back towards the entrance of the bridge, there he was again, Romey straddling his bike. That's a sexy look. I have to admit, he was nice and handsome in an innocent kind of way. Long story short, we exchanged numbers.

Getting to know Romey was a joy. He was a man of his word—he always did what he said he was going to do. And he always wanted me to be the best I could be, spiritually and everything in between. I loved that about him. Screwing around, trying to use or take advantage of me wasn't his motive. He was always in the mode of enhancing what was already in me. Financial wealth, literacy, and credit status were all very important to him, and he made sure that he helped me on the right path in those areas as well. That was one of hardest things to let go control of—I'd never let a man dig into my finances or my credit history at that point in my life, ever. I'd always been honest about how much money I made if asked but Romey wanted to talk to creditors, negotiate settlement offers, and help me get back on top financially. He had nothing to gain from that—he was well into the six figures himself. He never asked me for a dime, and I never paid for anything we were together.

There were so many things about him that I loved and he loved me for the simplicity I bought to his life. I knew how to treat a man; I knew how to play the part anyhow. But this was different. I didn't have to act; my guard was down. I could just do what came naturally in reaction to how I was being treated. I treated him well because he deserved it, and I didn't miss a beat.

One evening we spent the night together at my home in St. Louis. My house had the biggest pain-in-the-ass backyard you'd ever want to see... trees and leaves for days. Early that next morning Romey got up and left. I rolled over and went back to sleep...but soon after, I hear some banging, then an engine rumbling outside my bedroom window. I'll never forget what Mark said about men with good intentions—they will treat you well. Romeo had gone to his house to pick up his lawn mower to mow my grass. He didn't say anything or ask or mention it. He just **did** it because it needed to be done. As I stood there quietly watching him from my bedroom window, I just thought of how impressed I was—he wasn't obligated to do anything. Ordinarily, I'd pay the neighborhood kids to cut it. The point was, he saw a need and took charge. No need for me to control that or ask him why or take over. I watched him for about five minutes, just standing there. When I saw him I couldn't very well just climb back into my bed; I had to do something! So I made the man some lemonade and started to do my Saturday chores. It was about actions, not boasting about who does what and why.

At this point I was learning something new about being independent. I noticed most men are independent and they aren't talking about it. For the most part they aren't boasting about not needing a woman or how they can pay their bills. Why—because we expect them to do it naturally. Which brings me to the expectations men have of women—are we doing what they expect or what we think we need to do? Showing them the total opposite of what they want. I began to pay more attention to the actions of the men in my life and did a little less talking.

Romey had good intentions, and his actions spoke to that more than anything he could have told me and I appreciated that. I wanted to remodel my bathroom and decided to take on the task myself. After all, I'd seen enough do-it-yourself shows to pull it off, right? Wrong. After I'd torn up the bathroom where you could barely use it, Romey came over and saw the mess. I hadn't asked him for help, but he knew it would be a disaster had I tried to finish it. That man spent the next three days ripping out the floors and remodeling my bathroom himself. He told me to stay away from the bathroom. I enjoyed that. It was a relief and a turn-on at the same time. And it wasn't that I was "letting him be a man." I was learning to fall back and trust him to do what he said he would. To him it wasn't a big deal; that's just what he does. To me, it meant everything. As I paid closer attention to him, it was never about what I couldn't do; it was about what I would require a man to do once in my life. I had already demonstrated what I could handle if necessary, and from his point of view, if he was around, those things weren't necessary.

As the months went on, and our love grew it was so innocent and sweet. Romey was what I needed, when I needed him and more. When he saw something that needed to be done or if I didn't feel like doing it, and he could do it, he did it. And I didn't feel dependent or needy either. I felt even more free and independent but in a different way. If you ask him, he'd say that every woman should know *how to* be independent, but when she's with a man she shouldn't have to be. And not only was he right, he demonstrated it. He lived it; he was and is one of the greatest men I've ever known.

What I Learned

Fear, guilt, and shame are the devil's way of trying to seep into our minds and destroy us. For years prior to this, I had allowed him to do just that, leaving me emotionally vacant, bitter, and indifferent. I was too emotionally trapped to allow LOVE to get close enough to find me. I wanted to, but I didn't want to. I wanted to, but I was scared to. I needed it.

One of the hardest things for me was to let a man into what I had built, which wasn't much, but I was working towards my goals, traveling the journey on my own, and making strides in the right direction. And it wasn't perfect, and sometimes it may not have been the most ideal situation, but after so many years it was hard to allow a man to come into the picture and start marking his territory in my domain. I was only comfortable doing things my way up to a certain level. Straddling the fence, in a safe zone, no decisions had to be made there. I could teeter back and forth for as long as I could take being in limbo.

But that lifeline I mentioned taught me several valuable lessons. Those men may have had their own agendas, but so did the man upstairs. I learned that people are placed in your life for a reason. It's up to us to learn and experience what those reasons are. They both taught me how to be a woman and what I should expect from a man. Not only that, but that I deserved what I expected of them. I thought I had high standards and the right expectations in the past, but apparently not.

In the big scheme of things, no one thought I was needy but me. At least not in the sense that I think of when I think "needy woman." Men operate differently. They need something to do, to protect, to fix; it gives them value, puts more hairs on their chests. I had to learn to appreciate that and remember that it wasn't always about me. Sure, my ability to handle my affairs on my own was great and admirable in their eyes, but they also saw it was tiring. And I knew that to be true.

We like to think we always know what's best for us because we may have done a good job so far. But sometimes you don't know what you need until it's standing right in front of your face; then you'll wonder how you ever got along without it.

CHAPTER 10

I CAN PAY MY OWN BILLS
BIG DEAL, WHO CARES

It is easy to be independent when you've got money. But to be independent when you haven't got a thing–that's the Lord's test.

— MAHALIA JACKSON

This might just be one of the biggest badges of honor that many women wear. Money is power in the society we live in, and the more you have, the more freedom it gives you, and the more independent you think you are. No matter how broken, depressed, sad, or happy you are, in order to have power you must be in control of something or someone. You've been self-conditioned to believe the only thing that makes you independent is having the ability to pay your own bills—the ability to create and maintain a comfortable life for yourself, etc. Have we become so big headed as to think that paying a bill is as deep as our independent womanhood flows? Why, yes, we have. Like many independent women, I made my job my life, and my accomplishments defined me.

I never honestly believed independence was about money, no matter how little or how much of it I had, but that never stopped me from acting as if it meant something. In a lot of cases, paying my bills was the only thing I had control over. That's why it has so much power. And when no man is present, what other choice did I have, right? It's one of the first things that people associate with the term "independent woman." And for most, your mind-set is what set the tone and paved the way to you becoming an independent woman. Your thoughts turned into actions that made you finish school, work hard, get the promotion, win the contract, and so on, oftentimes before you made any money at all.

So why have we allowed finances to be the thing we're most proud of when it's truly a myriad of qualities that make you, you, and me, me?

Let's put this in perspective. If you lost your job or your business folded today and you had to collect unemployment or dip into your savings until you bounced back, would that make you any less freethinking today than you were yesterday? Would your independence be stripped at the moment your financial status changed? I'd like to think the answer to that question is NO. Seems like you'd be just the opposite—perhaps even more so. You would have to be more resilient, creative, and multidimensional than other women with a secure 9-to-5. Many would argue that the fact that you ever "needed" anything implies you were never independent to begin with, but I'm not convinced. You would begin to adapt in other ways to ensure that the essentials of your life were handled just as they were before. You would find yourself in survival mode, being even more creative. Does your paycheck determine your strength, your creativity, or your resilience?

I must confess...

After I'd been in St. Louis for about a year, I interviewed with a medium-sized, successful real estate company for a position as a general manager for one of their St. Louis properties. The position had been offered to others in the company first, but no one wanted to manage the

St. Louis market. The property was in major need of stabilization, staffing, and an overhaul of the morale of the residents. I was the fifty-third person interviewed for the position. I interviewed with the regional manager at lunch, and then they flew in the president of the company that evening for his stamp of approval. I was hired the same day of my interview, and I took pride in being the best at whatever I sought out to accomplish in that position. And out of thirty-five properties across the country, I was the second-highest paid in my position. That was a major accomplishment for me, especially since I didn't have a college degree. I was making just as much money or more than my friends and family members with degrees at that time. It was also the most money I'd ever made since my working life began at age seventeen—that was a long way from my first job working at McDonalds making $3.80 per hour.

I worked my behind off for that company. My team and I stabilized the property within months of me assuming my new role. I gave that position everything I had. While I was working there I obtained my real estate license and purchased two properties—one for the purposes of investing, to rehab then sell, and the other was my first rental property. I was very good at it and enjoyed it. Life was pretty good, financially. Nick and I were together during this time. I let the money I was making dictate every-thing—all the decisions I made were associated with money. Like most of America, money directs our mood, attitude, neighborhoods, schools, cars, what cable package we have, and our mind-sets. And like I said earlier, I didn't *really* believe it made me more independent, but once Nick and I broke up several years later, I did fall into the whole "I'm Miss Too Damn Independent" mode.

After about three years of dedication (2007), I was blindsided and fired from that position. It was like on Monday, I had it all, and on Tuesday the rug was ripped from under my feet. I remember sobbing in my office, and, to make matters worse, I had literally just put a contract on a new house just a couple of months before. I was devastated, and then there was the icing on the cake: I wasn't terminated for job performance, I was fired because months prior I had dated a guy (Chris), then his brother (who worked for me) witnessed a crime in another state. For some reason, the police thought I knew where he was hiding because I was his boss—and I had absolutely no clue! If that didn't make sense to you, you're not alone. The incident had absolutely nothing to do with me. Just the week before this happened I was told by the RVP how great I was and to keep doing what I was doing. But suddenly on Tuesday I was a potential "liability." I was pissed, more than pissed, actually. It was total bull but life had to move on. I had broken up with Nick just months prior so my income was all I had at that point.

My biggest mistake was that I made my position and my perceived "status" the focal point of my life, which left me actually *depending* on it. As if I didn't exist without it. Financially, I wasn't prepared to not have a job for more than three months. That means you're broke. I was more upset about *that* than being fired. I'd blown so much money on nonsense over the years—I was disappointed in me because I was smarter than that. I most definitely could have made better financial choices. I was so wrapped up in being able to do whatever I wanted without money being a factor; when it was gone, I felt like the world had come crashing down on me. I knew what financial struggle was as a single parent and I never wanted to be broke again. I was afraid of it, actually.

As the weeks progressed, I couldn't understand why this was happening to me and why finding a permanent position in my field was such a challenge. Nothing came fast enough or in the way I would have wanted as far as a job. It was discouraging. I was one of the best, so this time period had me doubting my abilities professionally. I found myself suddenly in known but forgotten territory; financial struggle.

After some dead-end leads and temp positions, I was open to almost anything. I was too stressed out to be independent! One day after speaking to my best friend of fifteen years, Kita, who lived just outside of Atlanta, I decided to pack up whatever would fit into my 2004 Monte Carlo and move to Atlanta. She and I agreed on some terms, and within three weeks I was on the road. Whatever didn't fit into my car didn't make the trip. I wasn't sending for anything to be shipped later. I didn't care, and I barely told a soul I was leaving.

At the time this happened I was with Romey—leaving behind him, my life there, my houses, and everything in them. I never was the type of person who was attached to material things, so I sold what I could and gave away the rest. "I'm outta here," I said! I didn't know what I was going to do, but I knew I was done with St. Louis. I didn't know if moving would fix anything but I was willing to give it a try. I viewed it as an opportunity to make a fresh start. Operation "Aprille, get your shit together" was in full swing. I was good at bouncing back from any situation, as I had in the past—I wanted this to be like one of those times.

Thankfully, school was out and my daughter was already with my parents for her summer vacation. I thought this should be an effortless transition. Move to Atlanta, get a job, save some money, find a place, and bring my daughter up by the time the school started again in the fall. Paper perfect. Shhhh, yeah, right.

You want to make God laugh, tell him your plans.

This situation really made me look deeper into who I was as a person, what was important, and it also gave me a lesson in what I **allowed** to define *me*. I had always thought of myself as a humble and giving person; I was the one people called when they needed something. I donated my time and money to charity. But evidently there was a lesson to be learned that I didn't see at the time. I believe God had something much bigger than I could've imagined in store for me at the time. All I knew was I wished he would hurry up; I was losing the little faith I had and was tired of people telling me to pray about it. I am so thankful you only need faith the size of a mustard seed to remain in his good graces because that was all I had.

The Truth

We've allowed money and other successes to be the focal point of our lives, because what else is there. Your job or career does not define you, it's not who you are, it's what you do. And the truth is, nobody cares how much money you're making except you and maybe a few of your so-called friends. And their only real concern is that you can "keep up" with them and the façade they're putting on. Sure, men want a woman who can contribute to the household, but your success to him isn't primarily money. Most men aren't concerned with how much money you bring in. He could be a millionaire and you a teacher, and as long as you're giving him what he needs, that's what matters to him. It's all the other things that make relationships important to men. The money only matters to you because you feel powerless without it.

There are women every day working hard, volunteering, and providing services to folks in need, not making a dime. Women building businesses that aren't turning profits, yet they're taking out second mortgages and loans they don't know how they'll pay back because they have a vision or an answered prayer. There are women leaving the workforce to help family members and making sacrifices some of us know nothing about. There are military wives thrust into independent-woman situations and single parenthood because their men are at war. There are women who have been physically disabled by degenerative diseases, but have spent the last few decades making a contribution to the society we are allowing to be destroyed. You can't tell these women they aren't independent. And in my book, self-sufficiency doesn't cut it when you add in a child/children and the responsibility of others in the mix.

The reality is, women as a whole are much deeper than writing a mortgage or rent check, paying our car notes via auto draft, making donations to charity, going to church, and feeding our children three meals a day. You could live your life on autopilot for years, pay all of your bills on time, and still not consider yourself an independent woman. Which is perfectly fine. The point is, it's not solely about the financials as much as it is about you *below the surface*. One thing couldn't possibly define who you are, so stop letting it. Just like you can't gain thirty pounds from eating one cheeseburger. It's all the cheeseburgers and fixings combined that makes our hips spread and booties jiggle.

PART THREE

Recharging Me

CHAPTER
11

THE RELATIONSHIP IN MY HEAD
SUBMISSION, CONFUSION & DREW

Nothing hurts more than realizing he meant everything to you,
but you meant nothing to him.

—UNKNOWN

Was there ever a time when you were tired of running your life and trying to run the lives of those around you? I've had many. The quick, decisive, savvy, innovative, go-to woman that I once was—was fading into the darkness, and I wanted to let it go, give up, take a hiatus. I was desperately in need of a release, a break, or a timeout. There were many periods in my life when I stopped living and began to exist in order to survive. "Submission" isn't the first word that comes to mind, especially after taking a vow of "I can do this on my own" rhetoric for so many years. It was always in the back of my mind, but that's for weak women, not women who are progressive and have it all under control.

I'd learned a few new lessons about not being so damn independent and just enjoying the things I was already blessed with. Truthfully, I didn't want to be in charge anymore. I was tired. I wanted someone to come and rescue me. Not necessarily financially, although that would have been nice, too, but just pick me up and allow me to do nothing—be in charge of nothing. I didn't wanna worry or stress about goals, achievements, or the next big thing. I just wanted to wake up in the morning and be free to be me.

Ahhh—welcome to Atlanta...

I must confess...

My best friend, Kita, and I have a post-hanging-out ritual of fourteen years: the Waffle House. Any location will do after a night of dancing and partying with the best of them in Atlanta. This night was no different.

We stumbled through the doors around 2 a.m., sat at the bar, and ordered our food. No menu needed! That'll be an All-Star with bacon, grits, raisin toast, and a waffle...please! At a table nearby are two men looking in our direction. We strike up a nice down-home conversation with them from across the bar. Moments later, they asked us to join them, and so we did.

As we're waiting for our food, a little small talk ensues between the four of us. Drew was from my hometown and so was his friend. The two of them were good-late-night company. Eventually our food was served, and as always it was worth the wait. We chitchatted a little more, and soon Drew handed me his business card. He was a local DJ.

"I occasionally need female voices for radio spots; can I give you a call sometime?" he asked.

What a great line, I thought to myself. I'm thinking, does he tell ALL the women he meets this? "Let me record your voice." We'll fall for that line every time, because who says that!

"OK, cool," we said in unison.

I gave him my number during the course of our meal. After an hour or so, Kita and I headed home to get some sleep! Drew was a gentleman and picked up our tabs. Sweet!

A couple of days later I get a message from Drew asking me when would be a good time for me to come to his studio. I was starting to feel a little under the weather, slightly scratchy throat and all, so I just saved the message. I just assumed I'd call him when I felt 110%. But he didn't give me the opportunity to call him back. Within a couple of days he had called me again. We spoke a bit and I told him my throat wasn't feeling the best, so maybe I'd come over in a couple of days. He insisted I sounded fine and that I should come over. So I went.

He lived just fifteen minutes away, so I told him I'd come over in about an hour. I'd been lounging at home in my pj's all day, so I hopped in the shower and started to get ready. I wanted to look presentable; after all, our first meeting was post-club, dance-floor hair and runny make up at 3 a.m. in a greasy Waffle House! I sent him a text when I was on my way. I didn't have any expectations other than a new experience in the studio and possibly making a new friend from my hometown. He didn't act interested at the Waffle House and there wasn't an immediate attraction on my end either; he just seemed like "good people."

Ding-dong. He opens the door.

"Hey, Aprille," he says.

"Hey, Drew," I said. "Nice to see you again. Hope my voice sounds okay."

"You sound fine...would you like a cocktail?" he asked.

"Sure," I said.

We headed upstairs to the studio, cocktails in hand. He'd converted one of his bedrooms into a pretty impressive studio with state-of-the-art equipment. OK, so he's legit. Sigh of relief.

"Don't be nervous, we're just gonna do a mic check a couple of times," he says.

"I'm not nervous…well maybe a little," I said. "What do I say?"

I was nervous, as if I were getting paid. I felt like Wendy Williams back when she was doing radio, with the big round microphone and hot lights in my face. This wasn't a date, but if it was, it would be on the top of my list of most interesting things to do, hands down.

"Ladies, ladies, ladies," he said. "Just repeat that so I can capture your voice."

"Ladies, ladies, ladies," I said, clearing my throat.

I sounded super country and couldn't stomach hearing my own voice! I'm not sure I have a job in radio, but it was fun. After a few other sound bites and talking a bit about his business, we headed back downstairs. We sat and talked for hours. He told me a little more about himself. This was the first time I really looked into his eyes and *saw* him. Drew was a handsome forty-something-year-old, very laid back, with grown children and his own business. He owned his own home and was newly single since the summer. He wasn't looking for a relationship and he made that clear to me then, just in his conversation. I wasn't looking for a man, either, and was enjoying dating for the time being. We were on the same page. A companion, some excitement, laughs, and maybe some romantic encounters. I knew going in that any time spent with him would be just that. I was in male-brain dating mode anyhow. Nothing mattered, no feelings, no considerations or common courtesies. I was casually dating with no purpose at this point; just for fun and my own selfish enjoyments. I'd already played the "lost in love and desperation" role and I didn't wanna go there again. I just wanted to live freely for a while.

Something about the way he looked at me and the tone of his voice let me know Drew was used to having his way, very much a man's man. He didn't have an "it's my way or the highway" attitude, but I could tell he was running everything around him. I think it was important to him that I knew that from the beginning. He didn't say it directly, but he might as well have. Still, there was something appealing about his demeanor. And he had the most beautiful, soulful, big brown eyes…there was an attraction. He was very laid back and firm, kind of domineering, but not controlling—either way, he was refreshing. The type of man that would make you fantasize about making love to him based on chemistry alone. We talk for a couple of more hours and there was a sexual tension in the air…like he can draw you into him. I was intrigued and needed to get out of there.

"Thanks for having me, this was nice," I said as he walked me to the door. I didn't want to leave, but I knew I couldn't stay.

He was standing in front of me and then kissed me, and I kissed him back. Nice, sweet.

It Seemed Real

We were both in a transitional period of our lives. We served a purpose to one another. I wanted to free myself from all of the things I claimed I was proud of. I was sick and tired of being in control—being Miss Too Damn Independent. I didn't wanna care about anything other than what I was doing in the moment. I wasn't stressing over my goals, my next move, how much money I was or wasn't making. My experiences with Mark and Romey prepped me for this way of being. I wanted to 'fall back' but was still a little guarded and afraid to trust—afraid to get hurt again. Besides, submitting is for wives…or is it? How do you marry a man then suddenly become the perfect wife? Suddenly you submit, I don't think so? Seems like something you learn, something you're taught.

This was a good lesson for me in more ways than I knew. No one, I mean no one, understood this, but Drew did. I didn't even have to tell him—he just took me for what I was and, more importantly, for what I wasn't. It was like he knew what I needed more than I did. Not only did I need him at this time, but Drew was also in a vulnerable place after losing his best friend to illness about a year before we'd met. He had helped care for him during his friend's time of need and was beginning to think about life—his life—differently. We were two very independent-thinking people who depended on each other for something specific; it was unspoken, and I believe we both had different, selfish motives—and that was okay.

For the first couple of months we were together almost every day of the week. I found myself spending as much time with him as I could, as he with me. I was attached to him—his voice, his touch, and his masculinity. We rarely left his house, and I must admit it was the most relaxing time I'd had with a man in a long time. I needed it. I wasn't engaged with a million little projects or ripping and running through the highways of Atlanta, I was just with Drew. On the occasions I would go home to give him some space, he would talk me into coming right back. We'd spend an hour on the phone going back and forth like high school kids deciding on whether or not I was coming back for the night. He usually won.

As the days turned into weeks and weeks became months, in my heart I knew I was beginning to have strong feelings for him. It took me a few months to admit this to myself because I was tired of going down this road only to have it end up a dead end. Not only that, he'd already expressed he didn't want to be in a monogamous relationship from the get-go. This was a hard pill to swallow, because he never once treated me as if he didn't. I always felt like he put me first.

I don't know if he knew it, but I was the most docile with him that I'd been with any other man my entire life, not the aggressive woman I was used to being. A toned-down, calm, more peaceful me. I listened to myself during my time with him and wanted to know what it would be like to fall back and trust a man to lead. Something about him allowed me to be open and vulnerable in a different way; not only my heart, but my mind. A part of me just needed a man to say, "This is what I want, this is what you do, this is what I need from you, and trust me to lead you in the right direction." And it wasn't about major life decisions, it was the little things. The little things that I'd let get in the way in my past—things that really didn't matter in the big scheme of it. Drew was that man for me.

I admit, many times it was a challenge, and I held my tongue and thought about my words more carefully before I said them. And at times I felt like I could just explode from not having my way. It felt as though I was giving him too much by letting him have his way—then I realized I wasn't letting him do anything. Drew did what he wanted to do and he didn't do what he didn't want to do—my actions didn't affect that. I recall looking at him and cursing him out in my mind, then coming to the conclusion that I wasn't always right and I didn't have to prove anything. I wanted happiness and peace more than I wanted to be right or be heard. I already knew what that was like.

Sexually Drew was aggressive, uninhibited, and rough in the heat of the moment. The mystery of his sexual self was appealing to me on many levels, and I wanted to experience him in a way that would be special for us. The unknown was exciting. He'd make love to me and I'd get lost in it, as if he had control over my mind and my body. At times I felt like his climax was speaking inside me. It's hard to explain. I wanted to surrender inside and outside of the bedroom. I could tell we never went all the way there—even sexually he had too much control. He wasn't giving me all of him.

He always said he cared too much about me to treat me like he treated other women, and I believed that to be true. He never made me feel as if he didn't want me. Drew was sweet and loving, affectionate and caring. Emotionally, we were drawn to each other. He was everything I needed at the time. No one else could have been there for us like we were there for us. It was a special connection that only we shared.

❦

One weekend in December I was visiting my hometown just before the holidays. Drew and I were just randomly talking on the phone, like we normally did, and out of the blue he said to me, "Do you love me like I love you?"

I was a little taken aback, but relieved to hear him reference it. Wow, really? I mean, of course I loved him. I was just at his place that morning, so I'm not sure why didn't he say that then. And because he'd always expressed he didn't want to be in a relationship, there was still a large part of me holding back, not wanting to "go all in" for fear of him pulling the "well, I told you I didn't want a relationship" card out in the future. Then I thought to myself, was I confusing his love to mean "he wants a relationship"? Can he love me without a commitment? He was so hard to understand, and his communication was good when he would talk—but it was difficult to get that man to open up. It was like trying to open a jar of something for some dish you're making and you can't get the damn jar opened. You try everything but nothing works. You know that once you add just a little of it, it's going to taste so sweet—but it's hard as hell to get there! But the truth was, even with all of those realities, I did love him and simply responded,

"Yeah, I do."

And the conversation went on from there. I didn't really know what it was supposed to mean. I guess it just meant he loved me. But for me, love meant something more. By this time, I'd clearly expressed to Drew in plain English that I wanted to be exclusive with him. But he maintained that he didn't want to be exclusive. I believe that was a defense mechanism on his part—ya know, he could always fall back on, "Well, I told you I never wanted a relationship."

"Things are great as they are," he'd say. He'd ask me why I had to take an all-or-nothing approach to our relationship. But I didn't like feeling like he had to contemplate being with me if I was so great—I needed the title. I wanted to hear him say that I was "made for him." OK, maybe not that dramatic, but can I at least move into the "this is my woman" category? If this had been a friend in this situation I'd tell her "he was keeping his options open."

Christmas was just around the corner and we decided to exchange gifts. I didn't get too excited about it, as I knew I was still in the "special friend" department. Financially I wasn't on top of my game, so I just got him something simple. I didn't read much into it, but its always nice to exchange gifts with someone you care about and who cares about you.

It was a couple of days after Christmas and I was sitting Indian style in his bed like a kid, well, on Christmas morning. He handed me a black, white, and lime green decorated gift bag with a card attached. I opened the card first and it said something like "Merry Christmas to a special lady." I thought it was sweet. Then I opened the gift, and it was a beautiful silver watch. Very nice.

"I love it," I exclaimed. "You didn't tell me we were exchanging <u>real</u> gifts! I just got you something simple!"

"And I love it. I'm gonna use it right now," he said.

Were the dynamics of our relationship changing, or maybe he just noticed I didn't own a watch. I read too much into it, I know. Either way, it was a really good day. And with New Year's Eve just around the corner, I wondered if we'd be spending it together. So I asked...

"Do you have plans for New Year's Eve?"

"No"

"You wanna spend it together?"

"Yeah, babe," he replied.

So, we're not in a relationship—I merely play by his rules and we spend most of our time together. OK, so what *are* we doing? In my heart, I wanted him to be my man. I jokingly referred to my time with Drew as the "relationship in my head," but maybe it wasn't a joke.

New Year's Eve came like every other day we'd spent together. We slept in, he did some work, we laid around, and I cooked his favorite meal for dinner: Salisbury steak smothered in onions, gravy, homemade mashed potatoes, green beans, and biscuits. Drew loved my cooking, and because of that I loved to cook for him. We watched a bit of the Times Square New Year's Eve festivities on television, had a few cocktails, and made our own fireworks that night. What a perfect entrance into the New Year.

Changing the Rules

I, like many women, wanted to change the rules midway through our relationship. At this point I began to want more, and he wasn't verbally giving it to me even though we acted like we were. My feelings were stronger; the love was in the air, so being in a committed relationship was the next logical step, right? Not for Drew. I really wanted him to "claim me," if you will. But he couldn't or wouldn't; either way, he didn't. It was so strange because we were so open with each other on so many other levels. I knew he loved me, I could feel it, and he showed it. I didn't understand why he was so against being in a relationship if I was so great. So then the question becomes, "maybe I wasn't that great?" Hmph. I guess I'll never know.

At this point I had been a nomad for several months. I'd been refreshed by the freedom of being with Drew but needed to get to real life. And since he couldn't commit, neither could I. And while in Atlanta nothing promising was on the horizon professionally, I was keeping my options open. There was a short-term contract on the horizon and I wanted to take it. It was an opportunity of a lifetime and could lead to many future possibilities. I wanted to be with Drew but I wanted him to want me more than I wanted him. Staying in Atlanta to be with him, to love him, to create the best life we could for us and my daughter, was what I wanted in my heart.

But instead of saying that, I asked him, "Do you think I should take the job?" What I wanted him to say is, "I love you, Aprille, and I want you to find something here. I'll hold it down until you do!!" Something!

Instead he said:

"Take it if that's what you want, babe."

The look behind my eyes was so heartbroken. It was like in the movies when one person asks another person a question just to see where they stand, and then the other person says the number one thing the first person didn't want to hear. Man, did I lose that day. I knew nothing would make him move any faster than he wanted to. But that didn't stop me from *wanting him to*. I just said "OK." I wasn't going to further express what he already knew, because it would have made no difference.

God, why did he say that? How could I expect him to be honest with me when I was holding back just to see what he would say? What would I lose by letting him know that I did in fact want to be with him? But I'd done that already, so what would be the point. A little of that past fear was creeping in, straddling the fence—trying to stay in the safe zone, not wanting to get hurt. I have to admit women play just as many games as men. We're all hurting, lying, and expecting things that we are unwilling to do ourselves.

I accepted the thirty-day contract assignment a couple of hours away in Columbus, Mississippi. I figured the time apart would be good for us. Perhaps he'd miss me and realize that he can't have what we had with anyone else. The two-hour drive to my thirty-day assignment was a thought-provoking one. I could only ponder, was this the beginning of the end of us? I'm leaving and we were just getting started. Someone said absence makes the heart grow fonder; well, let's see just how fond. It's only a month.

And a long month it was. Each evening before I went to sleep, we'd talk on the phone. I'll tell him about my work stuff and he'd tell me about his. Some nights we talked a lot about everything, and some nights we didn't talk at all; we'd just listen to each other breathe.

On a couple of occasions I asked Drew to come visit me since I was scheduled to work seven days a week, but he wouldn't. This pissed me off to no end. I couldn't understand why I was always the one coming to see him or doing what he wanted. A clear reminder that that's what I signed up for. When I asked why he wouldn't, he never had a reason. He just wanted me to come to him, and I did, every single time. He never came to me. So I made a point of driving back to Atlanta to see him to "check in" within the first ten days I was there. This was an eye opener for me. I wanted someone who would do the same things for me as I would for him—no matter how big or small. Fairy tale deferred.

While away on my assignment, Valentine's Day weekend was fast approaching, and I knew I'd miss it but would see him the weekend after. I was getting my career back on track and couldn't let a man slow me down. (Wait, isn't that why we want a man? To slow us down?) Though I was slightly agitated with Drew for not driving to Columbus to see me, I got in my car and headed back to Atlanta for a visit.

Again, we exchanged gifts. This time I gave him something more meaningful to him: a pair of high-tech industry headphones I'd heard him rave about previously. He loved, loved them! Then he handed me a small, dainty box. I opened it and there lay a diamond necklace. It was beautiful, elegant even. He put it on me right away as I held my hair up standing in front of the mirror in his bedroom. It was more than a paper-perfect moment.

Drew was always there when I <u>needed</u> him to be, but not all the times I just <u>wanted</u> him to be. It seemed everything was a lesson with him. I'm not sure, even today, what his intentions were. Maybe he had none. I don't know. I kept asking myself, were these mixed signals or did I not understand the development of a relationship? A true friendship first. I was hung up on Drew saying he didn't want to be in a monogamous relationship. Was I focusing more on having a man or building a relationship? We spent oodles of time together, and if he was seeing someone, it *couldn't have been very serious.* But who knows. I allowed this frustration to become the focal point of our relationship. I knew from the beginning that he didn't want to commit to being monogamous because he didn't know if he could live up to the expectation that would set. At least that's what he told me. But, in my defense, I didn't expect him to treat me like we were in one either. Nor did expect him to say he loved me or treat me as though he did. Had it been just sex, I would have been able to deal with that better than falling in love with the man. Well, that's a different story.

The next time a new man tells you he loves you, ask him how. How do you love me? Does he love you enough to be monogamous? Does he love you enough to make the commitment that you desire? Or does he just love you enough not to disrespect you in front of your face. Make sure you both mean the same thing. Love and relationships mean different things for different people. This was definitely the case with us.

After that first contract in Columbus, I took a month off and spent some time with Drew and my family. I had already taken another assignment that would start in a month or so, this time to Oklahoma and for an uncertain amount of time. I knew when I signed the contract that Drew and I would be over soon. But I felt like had to get on with my life. We were on different paths, and I realized that who I was attempting to be while with him wasn't *all* of who I was. True enough, I wanted to not care, to not be in charge (all the time), but it's me. Being with a man who could accept that didn't make me not be me; it just gave me break from not being me.

The summer of 2008, we planned a trip to Jamaica, the first for us both. We went to Ocho Rios for a week. It was gorgeous. I could tell he had some things on his mind and wasn't 100 percent present, and honestly neither was I. I was thinking about my next move and my life with or without him. About getting back to all of the things I was tired of. Emotionally, I needed the downtime, and the trip to Jamaica gave me a chance to really reflect. Drew didn't contribute to that one way or the other. I loved him but I was beginning to feel restricted. I wanted him to either let me in or let me out. I had to realize and accept it for what it was. While he was teaching me how to submit through his actions and letting go of all of the things that had me bogged down, the truth was that I am who I was and I am who I am. And though I needed the opportunity to slow down and just breathe a minute, it was a seasonal period of my life.

The most difficult part about all of this was that I was willing to give up a part of who I was to be with Drew, and I didn't feel like he would have given up anything to be with me. I truly allowed myself to depend on him on a level that I had never done before with a man. He may not have known it, but I made many compromises to be with him. He was beginning to make me feel as though I was willing to do too much for too little in return. Which was a sad truth, because I knew him, I felt, on a level that I thought was special. Aside from that, I realized that I should not have to 'give up' pieces of myself to be with anyone.

Our *"relationship"* ended on a sour note, with him not returning my calls and me flying to Atlanta with little notice to be with him. That visit did not go well. I let him turn me into the "psycho crazy chick" for about four hours, a place I had vowed never to visit again since Ryan back in Nashville seven years prior. He called the police on me as I stood— OK, beat the door down in hysteria outside his home waiting for him to answer…embarrassment was an understatement. I felt super humiliated that night in a way that I have never felt in my life. I can't believe I let him take me there but I did. He wouldn't even face me to end **it**—whatever **it** was—which I thought was very cowardice on his part. Again, Drew always did what he wanted to, even in the end. What I was feeling didn't matter enough.

Puffy eyed, brokenhearted, and mad at myself for feeling like a fool, I got on the plane the next morning, never to see or hear from him again. That was the worst plane ride back to Oklahoma. And when he was gone so abruptly, a little piece of my heart was gone, too. I truly loved him. For months I truly hoped he'd at least call to say something, anything, putting some closure to the time we had together. But he never did even years later—until one day, out of the blue, as I was in the process of completing this book on January 5, 2011. I received an e-mail message from him that said:

Subject: I still love you
I hope you still love me.
Drew

My initial *thought* to reading this was, "Bullsh*t and why now!" At the end of the day, I believe Drew only cared about himself and his needs. I don't know if he ever **truly** loved me…and it doesn't even matter.

Lessons to be Learned

Initially after we split I just felt hurt, rejection, and disbelief. I admit that I am still somewhat baffled at the purpose of Drew in my life. I spent days, weeks, months, and now years trying to make sense of Drew and what we had. I've come to the conclusion and understanding that not everything makes sense and not everyone can be put into a box or explained to fit some ideal of what *should be*. Sometimes I think it was to show me how to just be a woman and fall back—learning to submit—even though we were not married. But then I think submission is a two-way street that men have turned into a one-way street. Even with that, I needed to be tamed, to calm down a bit, so that was a good thing.

On the other side of it, I think he had some internal demons that had nothing to do with me, which I believe prevented him from "going there" in a way that maybe he wished he would have today. I'll never know for sure, but what I do know is that for the time being, Drew was a lifeline. We all fall down, and when we do, God sends us someone to keep us occupied in the meantime, while he's working in the background and while our life is *under construction*. This person is seasonal, not meant for a lifetime. I think we forget that we are seasonal as well, not only the people that travel through our lives. We are placed in each other's lives to teach or show each other something only we can. I was trying to hold on to someone that wasn't meant for me to hold on to. Our time was done, expired. Drew's not answering the door that final night was God's gift to me.

I was evolving and it felt good, but I still had some growing up to do and God had some things planned for me that I didn't even know were just around the corner. Ironically, I've learned that we will always have growing up to do; it doesn't stop until we stop. Facing the truth about my life, owning my experiences and decisions was apart of my journey.

CHAPTER
12

FACING MY TRUTH

They say perception is reality and that may be true,
but know when it's a lie.

— APRILLE FRANKS-HUNT

The truth is—the truth only has one side. Perceptions of the truth are lies about the way we see the truth. When I look back on my life, it began like most people. As a child you have no to little control, and you are in many ways powerless. Today my response to that is, and always has been, to get over it. But what I had to realize is that while those things weren't on the forefront on my mind and I was successful, smart, and mostly enjoying my life, it was affecting how I made decisions in relationships. One of the most difficult things for me to do for years was take a moment and really look in the mirror. I didn't have much time for self-inspection even though I thought I had it together.

I wanted to know who I really was, what my purpose in life was, and where my Mr. Right was. When would my life finally come full circle? For years I thought I was always working towards greatness and being the best I could be, and in many cases I was, BUT there was still something more missing? I had to face some hard truths about myself before I could get on the path I am on today.

∘✕∘

I am often asked how I let go of the things that were a part of my past. And my answer is simply that I don't think we ever really let go of things. I think how important or unimportant certain situations were or are to us changes. The past was what it was—it's over. It lives because we breathe life into it, good or bad. And even though it may have been wrong and you may have a reason to feel the way you do, the fact is, you have to deal with it in order to get through it so you can move forward. Finding the lesson in all situations was my key to becoming my authentic self. I wouldn't change a thing.

> Let go of the notion that you can change the past. It is done, stop living in it. The longer you stay there, the more of your life's potential will pass you by.

I know my past and present contribute to who I am, but only in part; it's not my final story. It's all important; it's all relative, the good and the ugly. Those difficulties remind me that I can do anything, my options are limitless, and I have the power to control my destiny in all things.

Self-Worth, Value, and Respect

Two words—get some! For me, it boiled down to respecting myself, knowing I was more valuable than my past, and learning to value myself in a new way. Sure, intellectually I knew those things and, as you already know, didn't put up with much for long, but that didn't equate to self-respect, value, or worth. I had to learn to respect myself more wholly. I thought I was worthy before I truly was—at least not worthy of the type of man I truly wanted in my life. Once I began to change how I thought and was more careful with my actions, things began to come full circle for me.

My experiences in between the men in this book were pretty good. The lessons I took from Mark, Romey, Drew, and even KD were monumental through the years. Accepting the relationships for what they were was also very imperative for me. I was learning through the mistakes I was making in culmination with the things I already knew.

It was about how I felt deep down in my core. It was about what fueled my tongue, my thoughts, and decisions as they pertained to dealing with men. We teach people how to treat us in everything we do; work, home and our friends. When something doesn't feel good, I had to learn to cut it off—not doing so told <u>them</u> I would stand for nothing.

Be Real with Yourself

I lied to myself for years by believing that I was stronger than I actually was. It just felt better that way. I never wanted to admit that my weaknesses were men, my need for attention from them, and the fear of what might go wrong. Doesn't that sound crazy as hell? I can only laugh—now—at myself and how silly I was back then.

Desperation, the New F-Word

No woman in the world wants to admit to having desperate tendencies and doing things that people would deem desperate. I am no different, but since we're telling the truth—though I wasn't perceived as a needy, desperate woman and I was careful not to demonstrate that, the truth was that I *was* both for a period of time. I may have rarely given in to those urges, but they were definitely there and made a couple of unwanted appearances over the years. I was conscious that I never wanted to be that "chick." It's not who I want to be and it isn't who I am. The occasions when I allowed men or some situation to turn me into "that woman" I had to take responsibility for my actions. I couldn't blame them (Drew or Ryan), I had to own it.

This is why it was that much more important not to waste time or deal with situations that would make me lose my composure to that point. No human being can have that much control over me unless I give it to them.

Do or Die

I had to let go of the attitude that I had to "get him" before he could get me—and most of the time I did. Even though I put on a happy face and was mostly happy, I still entered into many relationships with the predisposition of "this isn't going to work" or "why is he so nice?" I say it time and time again now: you think it, you be it. Change your thoughts, change your life, and that's exactly what I did, starting with Mark. I want to add, I needed help with that. It wasn't until God stepped in and gave me that first lifeline of "goodness" that I knew Mark didn't have an ulterior motive to hurt me.

I also learned men have issues too! It wasn't all about me. I had to learn to pay close attention and be the type of woman that a man would want to tell his deepest secrets to and be vulnerable with. I had to put my feelings aside on many occasions. I can say with certainly that not doing this is a mistake a lot of women make. We don't listen, and we think the only needs that should be fulfilled are our own. Not the case. I believe this is why the men of my past still love me today: because I am more than the lover I once was. I listened. I am a true friend.

Need to Control = Fear

Trying to be in control of everything or everyone is grueling work. It doesn't matter if you are able to put on a happy face and be all things to everyone; when you strip down to nothing, you don't, really can't, feel that great about yourself. And that certainly rang true for me. The need to control everything says that I had trust issues, and I now know that to be true. Don't get me wrong; I had a very active and mostly fun dating life, but emotionally I felt I had to be in control. And the crazy thing is, I didn't really want to be in control. I would much rather a man take the lead. Don't get me wrong, I **am** bossy and a bit sassy. But I don't **really** want a man that I can control in the sense of being a controlling mate. And at some point, after unsuccessful relationship after unsuccessful relationship with these "great" men, I had to ask myself, "What am I doing wrong?" For years my answer was, "Nothing"—which meant I was the problem.

I have learned to fall back. I have the men of my past to thank for that. Less control = freedom. Freedom = happiness. Happiness = a better you. I like that equation much better.

I Didn't Deserve a Good Man—just yet

Let me first say, "good" is a relative based on how we value ourselves and where we are in our lives at the time. A *good man* to me five years ago may not be the same today. So, what is a "good" man or woman? It's whatever you think it is. And if "good" doesn't feel good, then it ain't. Increase your own value and your expectations will increase as well. No one can define that for you.

As I said, earlier in my single years I thought I knew the type of man I wanted, with little thought given to whether or not I was ready or even deserved such goodness. As women we think we are entitled to certain things just by having female parts and having a good job. Having a vagina, boobs, and a paycheck is not the end-all, be-all to attracting or keeping a good man. There are women out there that will tell you it is—but they are lying, too. Besides, I knew how to work that, but it wasn't working for me. Get beneath the surface of yourself.

I'm not so sure it's the responsibility of men to change their view of what they *think* we stand for without us doing anything to make changes. It's our job to make evident changes within ourselves so they will *know* what we stand for and what we will and will not accept. I had to be prepared to give him something as well. Remember that men have needs, too, and not just sexual ones. They have a mental list of desires they want in a woman just as we do.

Eventually I placed more value on myself and made the decision to stop acting like a woman in the street and start acting like I wanted to be somebody's wife. I **did** want to be married; I wanted the commitment. But my prayers for a husband didn't match with my actions. I was still out there serial dating and "being free." It all has to line up. Is your life lining up?

Some day's I didn't feel all that independent and others I was at the top of my game. I spent almost fifteen years trying to figure out who I was through men when they couldn't tell me a thing. In order for someone to know me or you, we have to be true to ourselves—and you can't be true to yourself if you don't know who <u>you</u> are.

Tomorrow is a new day for all of us fortunate enough to wake up and see it. A new day to correct past mistakes, tweak some things about yourself, and deal with some things about your own outlook on life. Your past does not define you. It is like your DNA; there are many variables. And any day is a great one to start being real with the woman inside you. Self-reflection can be hard, but living a lie is even harder. You no longer have to look the other way and pretend that life is so great because you have this car, that house, or that career. You new attitude will be much more defining than anything else you have ever done. Change your thoughts, change your life.

CHAPTER
13

WORTH THE WAIT
WHO IS JSAD THE KING

Soul-mates are people who bring out the best in you.
They are not perfect but are always perfect for you.

—UNKNOWN

At this point in my life I knew exactly what I wanted, and I had to make a decision to make sure my actions lined up with what I was praying to God for in a mate. I'd already made plenty of mistakes and learned from them. So I had to be true to myself. I had to face some things about myself and understand what I needed to change to make me a better woman. I played an important role in my past relationships; they weren't totally my fault, but I was the common denominator.

Not looking for anything serious, but open to it should the opportunity present itself. I renewed my online dating subscription with Black-PeopleMeet.com as I continued to travel with my business. I'd used it in the past and it always kept my social calendar, well, busy. I gave myself a thirty-day window to meet who I could meet and then I'd cancel once that month was over. I temporarily living in rural Oklahoma for work and didn't want to be bored. It was an interesting month to say the least. I went out on several dates but nothing too promising. So I went to cancel my membership and clicked the "renew for thirty days" link instead of the cancellation link. I was pissed. It wasn't the money; I wanted to be done with the online thing. It was like social media on crack; addictive, fun and frustrating!

I wanted to be free to be exactly who I was. Sweet, saucy, freethinking, a little bossy, independent me. I had to make a conscious decision and make a concerted effort to not let my need to prove myself or put up a wall block the blessings I so desired.

So when in Rome…

So when in Rome, well, you know the rest. I took advantage of that next thirty-day period. I got a "wink" alert from a JSADTHEKING— but no message—so I checked him out. He was handsome, and what I appreciated about his profile was that he wanted a woman who had lived life and had a bag to speak of, someone who was independent but could also support her man as well. I was thinking that was definitely me. I was intrigued, so I sent him a note:

"Hey there, how's it going…nice profile."

He wrote me back, and that was the beginning of our dialogue. He was unlike other men I'd conversed with in the fact that he actually asked me questions—he was grilling me instead of the other way around. I definitely respected it, because that's what you do when you get tired of playing games. You just want to get straight to the point. It also let me know that he was truly serious about his quest to find *Mrs. Right for him.* And yes, actions speak volumes—but you should be able to communicate your desires freely between the two of you as well. Men and women in general don't ask enough questions of each other; we have forgotten how to communicate all together. So JSAD was refreshing for me.

The first couple of weeks we played the instant messenger and inbox game. It seemed to be hit and miss; I was busy and, as he put it, he had things going on in his life. He was at a turning point, as he had found out just a year earlier that he may have a thirteen-year-old son. So by the time I met him he had just gotten the paternity test came back and he was the father. He'd made the decision to raise his son and wanted him to move from Georgia to Oklahoma to be with him. The woman he wanted had to be able to accept this new addition to his life, and the transition between father, son, and the new relationship. I gave him my number. I was interested.

> I was in the beginning stages of developing my own company while in Lawton, Oklahoma, at the time and wasn't quite sure where it would take me geographically. This is the same company that took me away from Drew, but, as you can see, it bought me closer to my bigger purpose in life. How about that...

As the days and weeks went on we continued our online communication, but my location was a concern for JSAD, and so he didn't call. I couldn't believe that; I mean, excuse me! I was a GREAT catch! I'd worked on my emotional self, my physical, and was very successful in my business. Life was good—and I was always open to love. It always felt good to give it a go. *I'm such a lover.*

One evening we were instant messaging and I asked him why he hadn't called me. He said he wanted a relationship with a woman who knew she'd be in the state and was more certain of her professional future. He wasn't interested in a long-distance relationship. And honestly, neither was I. I'd already done that with Nick, had chased Ryan all over the country, and was pining over Drew; totally **not** interested. Since my career plans were open and relocating was an option, my business partner/friend Nita and I discussed it. So relocating was always a viable option—I wasn't moving for a man *per-se*. I just told him the first thing that came to mind: "every connection doesn't have to be a love connection!" Classic. Insert evil laugh here, please! My phone was ringing before I could type my next line. I remember his voice that night…talk about sexy! I was all smiles on the other end of that phone; thank goodness he couldn't see me.

We decided to meet in Oklahoma City that weekend. I booked a room at my hotel of choice. I remember exactly what I had on—skinny, ripped jeans, a tank top with a cutoff jacket, and some black peep-toe stilettos. I was super hot. Since we'd only messaged and chatted a few times, I had no preconceived notions about JSAD, only that I wanted to meet him and see what he was about. I was a bit nervous, which was odd, because I am a confident person. We met in the lobby of my hotel. He was cute in a country sort of way. We went to dinner, saw a movie, and went dancing that night. He's a phenomenal dancer and truthfully can out dance me on my best day. He was a gentleman, and our conversation that evening just flowed. Back at my hotel, we talked until nearly three in the morning. He had to be at work in just a couple of hours. It was like tearing us apart as he was trying to leave. I watched him walk to the elevator from my hotel room door.

"Bye, see ya later…talk to ya tomorrow." The girlish lingering, too funny!

At this point in my life I'd stopped holding the men of my past over the heads of the men of the present. So I entered into each date or scenario as if the past didn't exist. While I know it's a part of what makes me who I am, I choose to allow that to be a positive influence in my dating life and no longer a negative one. I was also a smarter—and surer of myself. Being comfortable and loving myself first was a major factor in that.

That same weekend, he invited me to accompany him to his mother's house for Sunday dinner. I didn't have his mother's stamp of approval just yet; JSAD was a serial dater, too, so it wasn't "special" that I was having dinner with the family. With that being said, for the first month I was the "girl he met on *that* Internet." I hear I received the stamp of approval from his brother and childhood best friend; his mother's approval came later.

That dinner led to more dinners, dates, and miles burning between Lawton, Oklahoma, and Oklahoma City. I remember leaving and him playing the song by Raheem Devaughn, "Believe" for me. The words are priceless to me and so suiting…

With affection like a dreamer.
with patience and understanding.
like a teacher with a student, vice versa.
promise not to hurt you, not to leave.
not to lie, not to cheat, not to fuss.
not to stress, like the rest in your past.

Believe me. I ain't like most men.
I ain't like them others
you done dealt with in your past,
just have some faith.
that is all I ask, believe in me.
why go searching, elsewhere lurking
when you been hurtin' for the real thing.
since I'm here before your eyes.
let's make love till sunrise.

I be something like the rebirth
of love with a twist
it started with a simple kiss
what could be more precious
then the rebirth of love.
Believe in me,

Believe in me, just try...try.
Believe in me.
I got another way I want to tell you.

Lately I have been thinking
about this crazy world,
being one step away from war.
So tonight, baby,
I want to make love to you
Like this world is coming to an end,
and if we should die tonight,
in the next life
I'm gonna love you the same.
Ain't nothin' gonna change.

Just beautiful. His sly seduction tactics clearly worked because that December, we found a house in Oklahoma and started our new life plan together. Our children were a big part of this transition as well. I didn't allow anything I previously thought about men to get in the way of my potential happiness and feelings I was developing for JSAD. I didn't overthink it, analyze it, or listen to my mother. I did what felt right in my heart and what made sense to me. I needed a man who would accept me for me flaws and all—one who I could grow with—one who'd make me want to be a better woman, mother, and friend.

> Yes, I know you aren't supposed to live with a man before you get married—I am not your spiritual leader or your mother. Sometimes it works out and sometimes we do all the right things and it still doesn't. I'll let my maker judge me; I suggest you do the same.

Learning how to communicate with a man was SO valuable! As women we tend to want everything to be about us; we only want to be catered to, and for the man to know our every want without our telling him. Through the years I learned it wasn't just about me, even though it seemed as though it was and I even wanted it to be. We discussed all the essentials women often don't—finances, which of us would pay the bills, future plans, rules for kids, rules for the relationship, what would make me leave you, and more. What were relationship deal breakers? We didn't leave any stones unturned. I have exhaled.

Even though I was used to making all the decisions in my life, I consulted him on mostly everything—the house furnishings, what insurance company to go with, and all the little things that independent women don't usually ask for guidance on. We did everything together. It wasn't that I wasn't capable, and I wasn't "dumbing myself down," but I learned that a man's input on what affects him is just as important—it's not all about what Aprille wants. I learned that a man will give you everything you want in the world if 1) he loves you and 2) you treat him like a king and respect him. Oh, and learning to shut up sometimes is real helpful too—women in general talk too much. We don't have to say everything we're thinking. Sometimes those thoughts are meant to be just that, thoughts in your head!

The First Year is a Test

The first year of any relationship is all about learning each other. What makes you tick and what ticks you both off? Respect is the main component. You won't like everything about him and vice versa! There are things I learned about JSAD that I didn't like, but they were not *deal breakers* so I learned to ignore them and after a while, those little things didn't get on my nerves.

The Proposal

I picked the ring so I knew the proposal was coming. We discussed the desire to be married early on. My thirty-fourth birthday was coming up and I was hoping he'd propose on that day. I was getting on my friends' nerves because I knew they knew what the plan was. Little did I know, he threw me for a loop and didn't ask on my birthday! I was disappointed but I didn't let him know that. I was like, OK…I need to not be in control and just wait, like a kid in the back seat of the car on a long road trip! I know we're gonna get there, but when!

It was a Sunday and we were headed out to go dancing, which we usually didn't do because work comes early on Monday mornings. At that time we had custody of two of my younger teenaged brothers and our two teenagers. Yes, that equals four teens in the house at once. They were all in the family room, which was odd because rarely are all six of us in the family room unless we're eating or watching a family movie. I dismissed it as them being weird teenagers. As I was walking into the dining room, it was like "lights, camera, action." Everyone had a role. My brothers had the camera phone and my daughter had the video camera. Steven (JSAD) gets on one knee, grabs my left hand, and says:

"I've been trying to wait for the right time to do this all week…Aprille, will you marry me?"

Of course I said, "YES!"

More than getting married, it was more about the feeling that someone chose *me*, wanted to marry *me*, and that God had connected me with the right man. I couldn't have dreamt a better man. Those other experiences were necessary so I'd know the real deal when it presented itself—so I'd appreciate them for what they were. Five or ten years ago, I would not have been ready for the proposal I received that evening.

It was never about the diamond (though oh so lovely) or a lavish wedding. The ring was for the world to see, the wedding was for our parents and families, and the man—well, he was for me. I wanted to be with the right man for my daughter and me. For the right reasons. I knew what loving for the wrong reasons was, and I was over it.

We were married just six months later in the fall. It was an intimate garden wedding with thirty of our favorite people. I wanted to be outside as close to the heavens as possible. We didn't have a bridal party aside from our children and a flower girl. I was so thankful and have been to God my whole life. This day was the most peaceful and perfect day.

We spent the next seven days in Puerto Rico enjoying the "us" that we'd already begun to build nearly two years before.

He's the best husband ever...a King indeed and I mean that with everything in me. He was definitely worth the wait.

Don't do it!

If you are with a man and the relationship is horrible **now**, for goodness sakes don't marry him. Put on your big girl panties and move on. Broken relationships don't heal because you say "I Do" at the alter and spend a crap load of money on a wedding where everyone there is wondering why in the hell your getting married in the first place. Everything we put together isn't meant to be together—and sometimes that means the people in our lives.

The Difference this Time

It's simple really—the difference was me. What I was willing to accept in my life and making the decision to be real with who I was were the best choices I ever made. God took me seriously when I began to align my prayers with my actions. The culmination of my past experiences with the men in my life and knowing that I was always being watched by the man upstairs taught me so much about myself. I am happier now than I have ever been, and my life would not be the same had I done anything differently. I accept the past for what it was and choose to embrace all of the lessons I've learned. The future is oh so bright and I am elated about it.

So more than being an independent woman, though I know in my heart she's a part of who I am, I strive to be more of a Virtuous Woman every day of my life.

CHAPTER
14

RELATIONSHIP DO'S AND STOP IT'S
THE ESSENTIAL EIGHTS

Get down on your knees and thank God
you are still on your feet.

—IRISH PROVERB

Now, this book isn't about finding Mr. Right, my intention is that you learn from my mistakes and experiences. It's also not about men and their issues, and we know they have some as well; it's about becoming the best woman you can be.

Your independence is in your attitude, your thought process, how you handle your affairs, in the clothes you wear, and, for the new generation, it's in your swag. It is <u>not</u> to be flaunted or continually beaten into the brains of others, especially men. It exists because *you* exist. It flourishes because *you* nourish it with your character, good or bad. Whether this shines through in a positive or negative light is up to you.

Through all of my experiences what I've learned is relationships are about respect, self love and a little selflessness. Here are my Essential Eight relationships tips.

#1 FORGET THE BLAME GAME
It's time for you to step up to the plate.

No more blaming or male bashing. Stop saying they're aren't any good men out there because that's a lie too. The reason it appears that there aren't any good men is because you are speaking life into that and so it is your reality. Work on you. Avoid putting yourself in the dating realm at all if you're not willing to come to terms with the truth. And yes, that takes work on your part.

Let the truth be told—we're responsible for a large number of men and why they do things that aren't acceptable to us because we have issues that we refuse to admit to ourselves. Then have the nerve to wonder why our relationships are unhealthy and filled with turmoil. Now those same men, in the same dating pool from five, ten or fifteen years ago are loose in the street and have it all wrong because we forgot to put some value on our so-called Womanhood. So instead of taking responsibility we now blame them for everything. I'm done blaming—I take responsibility for my part and so should you.

If you have past issues and have accepted things you know you shouldn't have, own it. We all have been the fool. When we put up with the crap from men it's because we have allowed it—then they leave the relationship thinking "that must be ok" and test the next woman. Sure, it's easier to continue dealing with something/someone that isn't good for you as opposed to going thorough the pain of looking in the mirror and the process of healing. But the time of dragging it out to put off the inevitable is no longer acceptable—let that mess go. You have no one to blame but yourself if you are a relationship mess.

#2 FORGIVENESS
Letting go of the past is the key to your future!

You're entitled to be mad as hell about whatever you're mad as hell about. Acknowledge that you're hurt to yourself. Know that you're not weak, you're quite human. Acceptance and acknowledgment of your hurt is imperative to your healing. No one has to understand why you're hurt but you.

We've already established that while Bitterness is real, it ain't Sexy nor is it healthy. You will never be able to move forward or have a healthy relationship without first letting go of what could have been. The reality is—whatever happened, happened. And your past is over—when **you** say it's over.

You must be willing to forgive yourself for the past decisions you've made in your life. Let go of the bitterness and forgive those you have hurt or who have harmed you or your family. They will no longer victimize you into thinking they have any authority over the outcome of your life. Don't allow another day go by mad with yourself or someone else, because of some decision(s) you did or didn't make that's contributed to you where you are today. You are no longer than woman, she is dormant and **you** can commit to living, a new—recharged life.

Forgiving is the act of giving that person or situation to God so he can handle it for you. It's about you—not the other person. It's about letting go of what was or what could have been so you're saying you acknowledge it and are making the decision to no longer allow it to control your life. Forgiveness=Freedom.

- Pray and/or Meditate—I can't stress this enough. Give yourself at least 5 minutes per day in silence with your thoughts.
- How did you contribute—Ask yourself: How did you contribute to the pain that you were caused. Think of at least three things that you could have done differently within that relationship and vow to change them from today going forward. No matter whose fault it may have been, take responsibility for <u>your</u> own involvement. Even if you were "done wrong" there are still factors that you may now see more clearly than before. Once identified, reflect and begin to work on those areas. Adopt a fresh new attitude and embrace the process.
- Start Journaling or Blogging—Write it down, get it out of your mind and off your heart! By journaling you'll have written proof your patterns. When ever you feel the need to vent, write it down or blog it!
- Closure— Understand and accept that your relationship was more than about you and the closure you're seeking – and that you may never get any closure from the other person. Closure for them may be not giving you the closure you need. For them, *this* may be closure. You may need a face to face, a phone call, or a response to your email messages. You want answers he isn't willing to satisfy you with. So, write a totally honest letter saying all of the things you want to say to this person. Not in the accusatory or hateful tone you may be tempted to but do be honest. It's up to you whether

you mail it or not, the point is—to get it off your chest and be satisfied with that piece of closure that you've given yourself.

- Seek Professional Counseling—If you're feeling stuck and can't seem to move forward on your own, sometimes the best professionals that can help you through a difficult situation is a licensed/certified counselor or coach. They can offer a non biased outlook in regards to your situation. A therapist can help you unveil underlying factors you may be having as well. Ask your family doctor for a referral.

Your **new** attitude is more important than your past ever will be. No matter what life has put in front you or how you have behaved, any decision you may have regretted is irrelevant from the point you decide to embrace a new attitude about your life, its direction and your new mindset. Gone are the days that you will be ashamed and be held responsible for what you have already forgiven yourself for. Today can be the first day of your newly recharged life.

#3 YOU CAN ONLY CONTROL YOUR ACTIONS

You can't change a man, period. If you think you can, you're being dumb.

Stop wasting your time with a man you want to change. The only person you have control over is the woman in the mirror. Many women knowingly make this mistake when we know intellectually that we can't change anyone. If your with or meet a man who is showing signs that he's not ready for what you want or has *told you* he's not ready—you have one of two choices 1) move on or 2)except it for what its worth and don't complain about it when he shows you better than he told you.

The first choice is your best option, the less time you waste on him the more time you'll have to run into Mr. Right for you. Put "Honey or Baby Boy" out of your house and stop letting him drive your car! But if you haven't learned your lesson yet and need to get spanked just one last time, the latter will be you. Don't complain about his actions and lack of commitment when he does things to piss you off—then falls short in some way. Be a big girl and take it in stride.

#4 BE OPEN & READY TO RECEIVE
A closed heart won't get fed.

Once you've reached the point where you're ready to reenter the dating arena—don't enter into it half heartedly. Allow yourself to be vulnerable enough to let someone in; it is the essence of a healthy relationship. If you block his attempts he won't get to the real you—he'll only have bits and pieces of the true you. And if that's the case he can't love you wholly, or in the ways you truly want or need. You have the right to protect your heart but you also have the right to true love finding its way into the nooks and crannies of your heart that haven't been explored by any other man.

#5 STOP DATING YOUR GIRLFRIENDS
Take the challenge and go it alone, like a Diva ☺

No doubt, you can't live without your girlfriends. As a single woman in many cases your friends are the only life line you have; which is great but that's not where you want to be every weekend. It's a comfortable place to be and you may depend on each other for entertainment, for something to do, a reason to hang out but often times you'd rather be in the company of a good man. And the times you do get together "men" is one of the hot topics on your list. And while they may mean well, they can unintentionally keep you in the same place they are in. Single. And *if* you're at a point where you want something more, you have to change up what you've been doing. And aside from that, when you're with two, three, four or more women—men have *too many* choices between all of you. It's like picking a cupcake out of a dozen, they all look tasty. It's too easy for *you* to get left out, not picked, like the kid who gets picked last for the baseball team or not at all. Don't be that chick. Create a new social circle—YOU!

❧

Switch it up

When you frequent the same places week after week, month after month—you have a higher chance of seeing the same men over and over again. Since you **are** your new social circle, for one month, each week get all dressed up and go out <u>solo</u> to a place you've never been to. If it's not something you've done before, it'll be a definite confidence booster. A man always notices a nice looking woman sitting by herself; he'll be intrigued and many times will ask "are you alone" or "can I sit here"? Even if you're not interested, make conversation with him and let him know you admire his confidence for approaching you. You'll learn something about yourself in the process. Just try it and see what happens.

> Men don't have the "go in a group" complex like many women do. Single men go out alone all the time in hopes to meet a single woman just like – YOU☺.

#6 YOU CAN'T LET A MAN BE A MAN
So stop trying! But you can learn to be a better Woman.

You've often heard the phrase "let a man be a man." And I understand the basis of that statement but I can't stand it. I think we are putting too much emphasis on <u>letting men be this</u> or that when we just need to remember or relearn how to be more womanly. More connected, more supportive to our men. Let's not over analyze it and miss the primary message. Be the woman he needs you to be so that he can be the man you know he is. But know that it's more about you trusting him enough to handle what you really need him to take care of and his word.

The men out there that you would consider to be a good man or catchneeds no verbal instructions from you on how to be a good man. Naturally, if you're in a healthy courtship or relationship—you both will grow and hopefully bring out the best in each other as you progress. Focus on doing your part in the relationship and being with the right man *for you* and if he loves you, he'll do his part as well. On the other hand, if you've chosen a man who needs hand holding, instructions, guidelines and such on how to be a man; he is not for you and you may need to have a "keep it real, real" moment with yourself. You don't need a man in a box with a million little pieces, you need a whole man.

Leave him be

Of course you can do <u>almost</u> everything a man can do but that's not the point. Don't try to prove you can do it too. Let that mess go. Trust me; he *already* knows you are capable. Learn to relinquish the reins to your capable partner and trust your decision. Respect the fact that men and women were created to be different for a reason and focus on how those differences can compliment each other. Understand that we are not equals and aren't meant to be equal—yes I said it. If we were meant to be the same we wouldn't need each other for all of the different reasons we do.

There are something's that men just feel good about doing, because they are men. And it's not just the trash, its individual specific. If he likes to clear the table, wash the cars, fix things and sometimes break things—leave him be! Take The Cosby Show for example. Clair knew Cliff would tear up half the stuff he attempted to repair but she left him to it anyhow. And did you notice how proud he was—even when he had to call the repair man anyway, just to stand over the plumber to make sure he was doing right? There is nothing sexier than a man being proud to do something for his woman or family. We all have egos, stroke his every chance you get.

No more operating out of fear.

Autonomy~Surprise! It's not all about you

> Have enough courage to trust love one more time and always one more time.—Maya Angelou

It'll be all about you when you're dead, six feet under or sitting on someone's mantle piece. Until then, life is about relationships. From the time you were born until the time you die—you'll develop them; use'em, loose'em, love'em and hate'em.

You don't hear men running around telling women their independent do you? I mean, all of the things you've thought about independent women kind of coincide with what society tells us—and those definition's really do describe what we want the men in our lives to do. Take care of us, be assertive, aggressive within reason, stable, and responsible.

You no longer have to exploit your own ability to take care of yourself and/or your family. Just as you carefully watch the actions of a man to see if he is what you desire—so do they when it comes you. When you feel the need to express just how autonomous you are you've taken the fun out of them figuring out your actual abilities based on your actions. And truthfully you may as well have a banner letting him know just how afraid you are of being in a relationship and how emotionally unavailable you really are. You've just told him in man translation "I don't need you, I've been hurt before and I run this." Loose the attitude as it hasn't worked thus far. If we didn't need men, and they didn't need us, we wouldn't have been created for that very purpose.

No one cares that you can take care of yourself more than you nor should they. Get below the surface and begin to peel back some of those layers.

#7 TALK TO HIM, THE WAY YOU WANT HIM TO RESPECT YOU

Learn to shut up when you should be listening.

Have you ever felt like or been told you talk to men as if they were a child? Using the tone of your voice to show him how strong you are. Speaking to him in a derogatory tone for no reason at all or yelling at him when he's not yelling at you. If you're a woman that does this in your current relationship, you should stop it. It's a total turn off and is **extremely** disrespectful. If you truly want him, don't drive him away with level of disrespect. He'll start finding reasons not to come home at night. No man wants to be with a woman who talks to him like a dog. You want the man you love and who loves you the melt like butter at the sound of your voice, you want him to give you his piece of the world. Speak to him with love, respect and admiration. If he doesn't deserve to be spoken to with such respect, why are you with him or you shouldn't be with him anyway.

It's takes a real woman to listen and then process what a man has said. When you don't understand or disagree with what he's said, don't bite his head off. Respond like the grown women you are. It's takes a little practice to learn that sometimes, just sometimes, you should just keep your mouth shut. It can be difficult to not give instructions or even take instruction from anyone, especially when you're used to *doing what you want* and not having to take others into consideration. Take it from me, shut your mouth and just listen. Most times, you don't even have to say a word. Learn how to communicate with each other with the understanding that we all communicate differently. Don't leave things to chance or misunderstandings.

A man will give you the world or break his neck trying to when he knows you respect him as the head of your household.

#8 THE JONES AREN'T THAT HAPPY
At the end of the day, do what works for you and your mate.

Relationships have many variables. Not one of them can fit into a box nor would you want it too. Forget the Status Quo—it won't love you back, feed you or hold you tight. Just like you're built from a special mold so is any new relationship you enter into. Don't get caught up with the status quo and what the Jones' are doing either. It's truly about what works for two people. What works for one couple, may not work or be understood by another and that is perfectly okay. What your parents, friends, neighbors or coworkers are thinking doesn't matter if you're <u>truly happy</u>. No one else can live your life.

Know what you will and won't except. Make sure you're reasonable in your expectations as no one is perfect. Then ask yourself, *what will work for me? What am I willing to live with or without—and does that or will that coincide with my partners desires. What are my deal breakers?* Remain positive in your wants.

If you want to be in a relationship—it's about what works for the both of you. At the end of the day, it's about you and your mate (family). Nothing or no one else really matters.

ENDNOTES

1. Mary Pickford, http://www.quotationspage.com/quote/31023.html, accessed August 6, 2011.
2. Cesare Pavese, http://thinkexist.com/quotation/childhood_is_not_only_the_childhood_we_really_had/154103.html, accessed August 6, 2011.
3. Maya Angelou, http://www.goodreads.com/author/quotes/3503.Maya_Angelou, accessed August 6, 2011.
4. Buddha, http://thinkexist.com/quotes/buddha/, accessed August 6, 2011.
5. Anne Frank, http://thinkexist.com/quotation/parents_can_only_give_good_advice_or_put_them_on/12719.html
6. Bertrand Russell, http://www.quotationspage.com/quote/1918.html, accessed August 6, 2011.
7. Plautus, http://www.brainyquote.com/quotes/quotes/p/plautus105244.html, accessed August 6, 2011.
8. Douglas Horton, http://www.brainyquote.com/quotes/authors/d/douglas_horton.html, accessed August 6, 2011.
9. The Luvologist, www.facebook.com/luvandrelationships, accessed June 2011.
10. Mahalia Jackson, http://www.brainyquote.com/quotes/authors/m/mahalia_jackson.html, accessed August 6, 2011.
11. Raheem Devaughn, "Believe" The Love Experience, Jive Records 2005. http://www.anysonglyrics.com/lyrics/r/Raheem-DeVaughn/Believe-Lyrics.htm, accessed August 6, 2011.
No copyright infringement intended
12. Irish Proverb, http://www.buzzle.com/articles/irish-sayings-and-blessings.html, accessed August 6, 2011.
13. Maya Angelou, http://www.goodreads.com/author/quotes/3503.Maya_Angelou, accessed August 6, 2011.

Aprille's Free Gift to You!

Made in the USA
Charleston, SC
22 January 2012